Practical Pre-School Books

Quality of teaching, learning and assessment in the EYFS

by Jenny Barber

Contents

Published by Practical Pre-School Books, A Division of MA Education Ltd, St Jude's Church, Dulwich Road, Herne Hill, London, SE24 0PB.

Tel: 020 7738 5454 www.practicalpreschoolbooks.com

© MA Education Ltd 2017

Design: Alison Coombes fonthillcreative 01722 717043

All images taken by Lucie Carlier © MA Education Ltd.

ISBN 978-1-909280-89-2

Outstanding
Early Years

Introduction

'Teaching is in every activity we provide. It is the summation of all that we do. There are no activities that occur in the setting which we do not consider to be opportunities for teaching. While we do not always know where these opportunities will present themselves, it is the skill of the adults that enable them to readily recognise the 'teachable moments' when they arise and respond to them appropriately.

However, it is just as important to know when intervening would hinder or stifle children's learning. Knowing how or when to teach is about knowing the child very well and being aware that important learning can be taking place without you there and without you directing what children are doing.'

Teaching and Play in the Early Years (Ofsted 2015)

Quality teaching, learning and assessment sounds to some extent daunting and not relevant for early years. Teaching and learning is incredibly broad and children are learning from the moment of birth as the process of brain development ignites. Teaching is the process by which we, as early years practitioners, support children's development through facilitating experiences and opportunities, sharing and communicating with them. Assessment enables us to identify if the children are learning, track the process of that learning and give us indicators as to how we can best support future learning.

The purpose of this book is to unpick what 'quality teaching, learning and assessment' means for early years settings, enabling reflection, developing understanding and exploration of best practice. Throughout, many examples are used from settings to help awareness of best practice and to support the process of identifying how to move forward and develop in your setting.

High quality teaching requires practitioners to:

- Develop understanding of how an individual child learns and what they are learning

- Accurately assess children's prior skills, knowledge and understanding and use this information to plan suitably challenging experiences

- Skilfully interact with children during experiences to extend learning with new words, ideas and challenges

- Provide the right environment to meet individual children's needs

- Build the right conditions for learning so that all children feel valued as individuals, safe and cared for.

All of the above points are explored in this book.

Quality teaching in action

In a 2-3 year olds room in a day nursery, the following exchange takes place:

Child: 'I need my telephone'
P: 'Why do you need a telephone?'
Child: 'I need my princess phone'

The practitioner reaches behind her for three pieces of luna park linked together. She asks the child will this do, as she demonstrates how to use the construction resource as a phone. The child responds eagerly, yes.

Here the practitioner was supporting the child to understand the idea of representation, through symbolic play. How something can be used to represent something else, an important concept in learning to read.

Quality teaching in action

In a toddler's room in a day nursery, a practitioner shows each child two coloured beaker lids. She asks the children to say which one they would like, encouraging the children to say the name of the colour, if they do, she says the name to reinforce that knowledge. If a child simply points, she says the colour name and encourages them to copy.

In this example, the practitioner is supporting language development and supporting freedom of choice for the children.

When high quality teaching is embedded in high quality practice and provision, it is the practitioner's skilled interactions with children which helps to move their learning forward.

As people look at things differently, you could end up with a variety of interpretations, which can only benefit good practice and generate thoughtful discussion.

To begin with, look at the overview of the good judgment for quality teaching, learning and assessment, considering how it might be seen in the setting and evidenced. The chart on page 4 can be a good starting point for reflection with your team in a staff meeting.

Encourage everyone to consider what they think each statement means, how that translates into practice and what evidence would support the implementation. This exercise can be useful for managers and leaders in settings to ascertain the practitioner's knowledge and understanding.

The provision is good because:

Descriptor	Reflection	Evidence
Practitioners have high expectations of all children based on accurate assessment of children's skills, knowledge and understanding when they join the setting. The quality of teaching is consistently strong. Practitioners have a secure knowledge and understanding of how to promote the learning and development of young children and what they can achieve. Practitioners complete regular and precise assessments of children's learning that they use to effectively to plan suitably challenging activities. They observe carefully, question skilfully and listen perceptively to children during activities in order to re-shape activities and give children explanations that improve their learning. Practitioners teach the basics well and support children to learn the communication and language skills and develop the physical, personal, social and emotional skills they need for the next steps in their learning. Where appropriate, early literacy skills and mathematical development are promoted effectively to ensure that children are ready for school. The key person system works effectively to engage parents, including those who may be more reluctant to contribute, in their children's learning. Parents contribute to initial assessments of children's starting points on entry and they are kept informed about their children's progress. Parents are encouraged to support and share information about their children's learning and development at home. Practitioners provide a wide range of opportunities for children to learn about people and communities beyond their immediate experience. Resources and activities reflect and value the diversity of children's backgrounds and experiences.	How do you demonstrate in practice that you have high expectations for all children? What methods do you use to identify children's starting points when they join your setting? How do leaders and managers ensure that teaching is consistently strong throughout the setting? How do they support their team in understanding how to promote children's learning effectively? How do you reflect on the different ways to use information from both recorded and seen observations of the children? Do you respond in the moment to children's learning needs and provide possible challenge and extension? How confident are practitioners in re-shaping activities? How do they use language to provoke and challenge thinking and therefore extend learning? How are the prime areas supported and do observations reflect children's progress effectively? Do all practitioners have clear understanding of the processes involved in mathematical learning and understanding? Are they all aware of effective support for literacy skills including mark making and development of phonic awareness if appropriate. How do you involve and engage hard-to-reach parents? How do you reflect the local community through the provision, broadening out children's awareness as appropriate? What do you access in the local community? Do you go out and about?	Starting points assessment, including reflection on prime areas, interests of the child and characteristics of effective learning. Clearly differentiated planning which is developmentally reflective of all children. A broad variety of teaching opportunities are utilised. Practitioners demonstrate an understanding of how children learn. The characteristics of effective learning are embedded and reflected through the provision. Clear learning plans in place for children with additional learning needs across the spectrum of needs. Provision of activities that are interesting and appropriately challenging. Evaluated planning, identifying learning and how to move forward. Clear next steps which are appropriate and meaningful and linked to children's learning and development needs. The planning cycle clearly in action both in practice and in the observation cycle. Practitioners skilled and confident in going with the flow and developing activities to reflect learning interest of the children. Practitioners using language to support and promote learning through the use of statements, open-ended questions. Are opportunities used for incidental mathematical learning? Parents make contributions to initial assessment. Clearly identified strategies are used to enable parents to support their children's learning at home, working together.

(Source: Early Years Inspection Handbook, Ofsted, September 2015)

Teaching in the early years

Teaching is a term that reflects and encompasses so many elements of what happens during the day. Teaching is not simply about planned experiences, but is about being responsive to the children. The ability to respond and teach should be innate and be present at all times, whether that is chatting to a baby whilst changing their nappy or leading a cooking activity with a group of four year olds.

The origin of the word 'teach' is Germanic and in old English means to show, present and point out. The old English definition is an interesting way to reflect on teaching in early years. We show, present and point out by modeling language, demonstrating, presenting the learning environment, using provocations and introducing and exploring new ideas. The broader the view we have of teaching the better, as this will mean that we are able to have a much more positive impact on children's learning.

In the *Early Years Inspection Handbook*, Ofsted describes teaching in the early years as follows:

'Teaching should not be taken to imply a 'top down' or formal way of working. It is a broad term that covers the many different ways in which adults help you children learn. It includes their interactions with children during planned and child initiated play and activities: communicating and modelling language, showing, explaining, demonstrating, exploring ideas, encouraging, questioning, recalling, providing a narrative for what they are doing, facilitating and setting challenges. It takes account of the equipment adults provide and the attention given to the physical environment, as well as the structure and routines of the day that establish expectations. Integral to teaching is how practitioners assess what children know, understand and can do, as well as taking account of their interests and dispositions to learn (characteristics of effective learning), and how practitioners use this information to plan children's next steps in learning and monitor their progress.'

Early Years Inspection Handbook (Ofsted September 2015)

So if that is broken down for an overview of practice, teaching in an early years context could be seen in the following ways:

- Supporting and developing independence skills at meal times and snack times

- Through story time and the variety of ways in which books can be used and explored

- Songs and rhymes, especially when props are used

- Leading well planned and differentiated adult led activities which enable learning and opportunity for extension of learning, both inside and outside

- Demonstrating at all times high expectations of children

- Provocations set up within the learning environment both inside and outside. Provocations that are refreshed and used with thought (see Chapter 3)

- The provision of the learning environment, with open-ended opportunities both inside and outside

- Innovative and interesting use of resources, including unusual and every day objects

- Being spontaneous and recognising in the moment teaching opportunities to extend learning

- Engaging in appropriate communication with children which is supportive of their learning and development. The use of different communication strategies, including modelling, the use of statements, open-ended questions and silence

- Having a routine and structure to the day that enables children to become immersed and absorbed in their learning

- Utilising opportunities in the routine for teaching e.g. hand washing, counting children, reflection

- Knowledge and understanding of the children and how they learn to enable clear planning which is supportive of their next steps

- Clear evaluation of the provision and children's learning through the experiences and opportunities provided.

However, it is also mindful to at all times remember this quote:

"Each time one prematurely teaches a child something he could have discovered himself, that child is kept from inventing it and consequently from understanding it completely." **Jean Piaget**

Our intervention and teaching need to be sensitive and appropriate for each child.

Perhaps it is easier to consider teaching in early years as best practice in supporting children's learning; expanding and developing their potential and feeding their thirst for knowledge. This can be achieved equally through something quite simple, as well as the more complex. Skilled practitioners need to be responsive to children through observing and listening carefully to what they are saying and, if appropriate, sensitively moving in and extending the learning by teaching in the moment. Here are three straightforward examples of spontaneous, in the moment, quality teaching.

Case study **Supporting language**

An 18 month old child is interacting with a practitioner handing her objects over and over, as she receives each object the practitioner says 'for me?' pointing at herself.

Why is this quality teaching?

This is quality teaching as it is demonstrating positive interactions. The practitioner is supporting the child to engage in two way communication, in responding both verbally and non-verbally to what the child is saying, reinforcing the meaning of the language with the gesture, connecting the two together in an affirmative manner.

This is crucial when children are in the early linguistic stage of development, the practitioner is therefore acknowledging and valuing the child's interactions, supporting and building the child's confidence in their early attempts at communicating.

Case study Building blocks

A four year old child is attempting to build an elaborate construction with oblong wooden blocks. He is trying to build along and up and is placing the bricks on top of each other narrowest and longest side down. His structure is unstable and collapses, several times. Each time it collapses he shrugs his shoulders holding his hands up in the air, but he perseveres and tries again and again.

After the fourth attempt a practitioner comes over to him and suggests he might find it easier if he places the bricks on top of each other with the widest side down creating more stability. The practitioner moves away, and the child pauses and reflects. He then follows her suggestion and discovers that it works, seeing that his structure is stable. He sits back and considers it for a moment and he then leans forward and blows the structure to test the stability and discovers it is sturdy.

Why is this quality teaching?

The practitioner can see the child cannot find the solution for himself, so responds in the moment by giving a suggestion. She doesn't take over or direct, just explains and then lets him continue for himself, knowing he is capable of following through with her suggestion, therefore demonstrating she has high expectations. She enabled him to make the discovery for himself to consolidate understanding and learning, which he in turn tested by attempting to blow the construction over. The child learnt through the practitioner intervention. As this is part of the continuous provision, the child would be able to revisit to consolidate his learning.

Is there an alternative?

For a child who perhaps does not have the same level of critical thinking skills, the practitioner could have worked alongside the child modelling the alternative way of using the blocks and then moved away, to enable the child freedom to explore. With a less resilient child, the practitioner would have needed to intervene earlier.

Case study Water play

A three year old child is playing in the water tray, filling up empty milk plastic bottles of different sizes. He carefully fills them up and then screws the lid on, he then holds the bottle upside down over the floor and shakes it to test if the lids are tightly screwed on.

A practitioner observes his play and says to him that in the cupboard, there are some even larger bottles and would he like to use them? He says that he would and together they go to the cupboard to get the bottles and return them to the water tray.

Why is this quality teaching?

The practitioner observed the child and identified that she could extend the activity for the child, with the larger bottles enhancing his experience. By asking him, she was involving him in the decision-making and direction of his own learning. It is also an example of teaching in the moment.

Is there an alternative?

Whilst not necessarily possible in the moment, depending on what is available, a broader selection of bottles and jars with lids could be introduced. The practitioner could also have used some careful questioning to support the child to reflect on, and articulate his thoughts on what he was doing e.g. why was he shaking the bottles upside down?

Quality teaching examples

Example	Why it is quality teaching
Children are using boxed pencil sharpeners and a practitioner uses this opportunity to develop knowledge asking 'if it is not full what is it?' indicating the sharpener box, where the shavings collect.	The practitioner uses an everyday opportunity to challenge the children's thinking and give them pause to reflect on the answer. It is also an example of teaching in the moment.
On a windy day practitioners spontaneously set up outside a kite making activity. When asked, the children were able to explain the wind was making their kite 'fly', having had the process explained to them by practitioners.	This is an example of spontaneous planning responding in the moment and capturing the children's interest.
Children in pre school are outside and encouraged to listen to the crunch of the frost on the grass and look at the formation of the frost on leaves.	Here the children are encouraged to consider frost in two different ways, its sound underfoot and appearance, therefore extending learning and encouraging reflective thought.
Play dough ingredients are set up on the table and the children explore how to make the dough, adding the ingredients themselves and forming dough through trial and error and exploring colour, the practitioner supports making statements about their explorations and asking questions.	The children were enabled to direct the activity for themselves and learn through their own first hand experiences how to make effective play dough. They were able to use their knowledge from previous experiences of playing with dough, to understand what they were trying to create. The process was effectively supported by the practitioner.
Following on from exploring torches, a practitioner sits under the parachute with a group of children using torches to read the story Funnybones.	The practitioner took the opportunity to extend and develop the children's interest in the use of torches to introduce a fun and spontaneous activity.
During a painting activity a practitioner discusses with a child how white paint makes the colour lighter.	The child had been exploring with powder paint, creating colours and exploring, it is supported by the practitioner explaining how white paint affects the shade.
Several children in the pre school room wanted to paint but only 2 children could use the easel. A practitioner responded to this interest by setting up table top painting, asking the children what colours they would like and encouraging them to squeeze the paint out of the bottles into the paint tray.	The practitioner responded to the children's desire to paint and therefore their individual needs by extending the provision and involving them in setting up the activity, encouraging independence and providing opportunity for the children to be involved in the planning.
A child in pre school at lunch time states that 'rice is nice' a practitioner asks him what those words do and he replies 'rhyme'.	The practitioner is responding and acknowledging what the child has said and encouraging him to reflect on his words and consider rhyming words. It is also an example of teaching in the moment.
Outside in a tuff spot, use flour, sugar and baking play, messy play with jelly and spaghetti. These activities are enjoyed by all children across the age ranges in the day nursery. The children were able to extend their own learning and engage in purposeful play.	This is a clear example of supported child initiated activity, which is provided so the children can access it at their own level and direct their own learning.
A child in the toddler's room is told 'clever girl, you used a new word today, orange'.	The child's use of language is supported and acknowledged.
At the play dough table, a practitioner is demonstrating how to make tiny beads of play dough, by placing a tiny piece of dough in her palm, and using her finger to roll. The children observe her carefully and begin to copy.	This is a clear example of showing modelling to support and develop children's understanding, and is supportive of fine motor skills.

Teaching in the moment

Teaching in the moment is about being immediately responsive to something a child has done or said, seizing the chance to develop and extend learning; this might be verbally or non verbally. It is important as children don't wait for the next connection to be made in their learning, learning for children needs to be in a meaningful context and the immediacy of this, is more significant the younger the child.

Teaching in the moment requires skilled practitioners to recognise the key moment and know at which point to intervene and would that intervention be of benefit to the child? Trying to understand it from the child's perspective. The child benefits as learning is specific, relevant and meaningful to them. It will tap into a curiosity, an interest or fascination. The teaching is effectively personalised, e.g. in the earlier building blocks example on page 7.

What you need to teach effectively

Understanding of how children learn and the process of child development and the relationship between the two	Children learn in a variety of ways and in different combinations and may change throughout the day. Some children's learning will be very much influenced by their current schema. As practitioners, we need to recognise learning styles and appreciate that access to experiences to support learning is related to child development e.g. the development of fine motor skills and hand and eye coordination.
Developmentally appropriate practice	We should have high expectations of children, to support them in reaching their potential, however those expectations need to be linked to their developmental capabilities. This is enabled through clear understanding of learning trajectories and the importance of consolidated learning before moving on.
Ability to listen, observe and respond in the moment	Observing and listening to the children taking cues from them as to how best to support their learning, perhaps by additional resources or supporting a change of direction with a planned activity.
Willingness to reflect on how to develop learning for children.	Every child has their own unique way of learning, to enable us to meet their individual needs we need to facilitate their learning. The child that mostly plays with trains, how can they be used to broaden learning? Could the track be present on a different surface at a different height, can engines and carriages be numbered, could challenges be set.
Patience	Children can't be rushed, everything needs to go at their pace, as they process and assimilate thoughts, ideas and concepts in their brains and they repeat and revisit experiences to consolidate, e.g. self help skills. Patience is also critical with language, as we wait for children to process the meaning of words and answer questions.
Empathy	Understanding of how a child is feeling has to come first. If they are happy, content and secure in that moment, learning is more likely to take place. The effective practitioner needs to put themselves in the child's position to enable a feeling of empathy. This is closely linked with The Leuven Scale of Well Being (see page 15).
Consistency	The practitioner needs to be consistent in their approach, mood and enthusiasm to give the child a sense of security and a feeling of stability with that practitioner to enable learning.
Inspiring	To teach effectively and to inspire the children you need to make an impression. That might be through your approach, your ability to laugh, to show that making a mistake doesn't matter. You want the children to remember you and what you taught them and what they learnt.
Creativity	To teach effectively you need to be creative in your approach and be able to adapt an idea or an approach to suit a child's interest or learning needs, therefore motivating them to learn.
To know what that child needs	Be able to consider and answer that question for yourself for each of your key children, knowing exactly what each individual child needs to learn.

These indicators for effective teaching, can be useful as prompts for observations of staff practice.

Sometimes practitioners can have a lack of understanding of the gradual process of learning, which can impact on planning and children's learning. Practitioners need secure knowledge of child development and the process of learning. Less knowledgeable practitioners need to be supported in their setting to develop skills and understanding.

In conversation (example from practice)

Discussing with a practitioner one of their key children, I asked her if there was anything in particular she was focusing on for the child's next steps. The child was aged two and a half. The practitioner told me the child was beginning to share awareness of simple shapes, so her next step was to develop the child's awareness of more complex shapes. I asked the practitioner what she defined as a more complex shape, she responded sphere, pentagon, hexagon and octagon.

The practitioner hadn't recognised the need for the child to be confident in her understanding and awareness of simple shapes within play and the environment and for that learning to be consolidated. Awareness of the complex shapes mentioned whilst they might be involved in play, would not form part of any teaching strategy until later.

Example	Reason
Stencils provided for toddlers mark making	Children of this age need to freely explore mark making using large chunky crayons or chalks that fit into their hands. They need large pieces of paper to enable freedom of movement of the arms. The development of fine motor skills is linked with the gross motor development of the arms and shoulders.
A4 paper and felt tip pens in a baby room	Very young children, especially babies need to explore paint, messy play and dough with their hands first to begin to develop muscle control and co-ordination before using any tool.
A practitioner writes a child's name on their drawing	If the child is able, they should first have a go at writing their name. The practitioner should model the writing of the child's name, so the child can see clearly.
A practitioner is encouraging children to make sandcastles with dry sand.	This is a clear example of a practitioner putting no thought into what they are doing, as obviously the child is not going to succeed and is effectively set up to fail. Additionally they are missing out on understanding the necessity for wet sand to build a castle.

Case study Snowmen

In a pre school a practitioner is leading an activity where the children are making collage snowmen, which involves cutting out pieces and sticking them together. Some of the children take time to cut so the practitioner says I will help you and then cuts it out for them. There is a glue stick on the table for the children to use. The practitioner shows the children where to stick each piece exactly, by pointing and sticking for them.

Why is this not quality teaching?

The adult is not demonstrating patience or understanding of the skills involved in cutting, by impatiently cutting the snowmen out. Creativity is not enabled as the children cannot choose where to stick as the adult is directing them, the use of the glue stick also means there is no opportunity to explore the properties of glue and develop fine motor skills. This activity had minimal learning for the children and they gained very little if anything from the experience. The practitioner had not remembered that the learning takes place in the process and the emphasis should not be on the end product.

How could the activity be improved?

The children could be provided with pva glue and glue spreaders, various collage materials and scissors, so they could create their own snowman developing their skills and demonstrating creativity in the uniqueness of their snowmen.

Ofsted statement (good criteria)	What it means / what Ofsted will be looking for
The quality of teaching is consistently strong. Practitioners have a secure knowledge and understanding of how to promote the learning and development of young children and what they can achieve.	Teaching, in all its forms, needs to be of a consistently high standard across the whole setting, so no matter which room children are in and which practitioner is supporting them their experience is strong. Practitioners use different methods to promote and support children's learning and respond in the moment to cues and prompts from the children. They have high expectations of what children can do and consistently encourage them.

How do we support children's learning?

So, how do we begin the process of supporting learning for children? It begins with the 'Unique Child', the understanding of each individual, what makes them who they are, their life experiences when we meet them, what they enjoy doing, their likes, dislikes, interests, their personality, in essence their uniqueness as a human being.

The **unique child** is surrounded by **positive relationships**, relationships which make them feel emotionally secure within the setting/school, building confidence and self esteem, which is in turn supportive of learning. Those positive relationships being child and key carer, child with other practitioners, child to child and modelled relationships practitioner to practitioner and practitioner to child's parent.

The **unique child** then engages with the **enabling environment** where their interests, development and learning needs are reflected. They feel secure as they are supported by positive relationships and learning and development will be enabled.

However, for the learning and development to flourish, we need to ensure the children are effectively supported in an environment that meets their needs and reflects their learning styles. We need to consider the needs of the unique child, and ask ourselves: are the children surrounded by positive relationships, is the enabling environment stimulating, interesting and challenging. Essentially is everything in place for learning and development to take place?

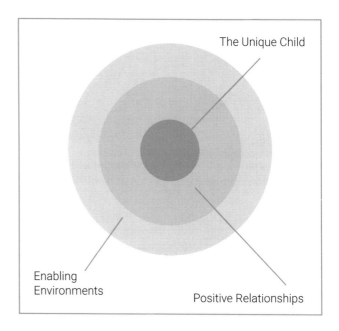

It is important to remember that as well as facilitating the positive relationships, the adult is a key part of the enabling environment and is as important as the resources. Children need interested and motivated adults within the environment. A child could be in an environment with the most amazing resources, but without effective adults who observe, interact and engage, the learning potential decreases significantly.

The characteristics of effective learning help us to explore these themes and in this chapter we will consider the Unique Child. Considering how the child may choose to learn and the characteristics they demonstrate, enables to be more effective in our support, intervention and the approach we may take.

The characteristics of effective learning – The 'Unique Child'

	Learning opportunity	For the child	How it might be seen
PLAYING AND EXPLORING - Engagement	**FINDING OUT AND EXPLORING** ■ Showing curiosity about objects, events and people ■ Using senses to explore the world around them ■ Engaging in open-ended activity ■ Showing particular interests	I am showing particular interests. I show curiosity about objects, people and events. I engage in open-ended activities. I use my sense to explore the world around me.	■ Messy play ■ Sand ■ Water ■ Body painting ■ Repetitive play with a particular resource/resources ■ Mud play ■ Fascination with mini beasts ■ Treasure baskets ■ Heuristic play
	PLAYING WITH WHAT THEY KNOW ■ Pretending objects are things from their experience ■ Representing their experiences in play ■ Taking on a role in their play ■ Acting out experiences with other people	I like acting out my experiences in play. I like pretending objects are things that I know. I like taking on a role when I play. I like acting out experiences with other people.	■ Home corner ■ Role play ■ Small world play ■ Play with everyday objects ■ Demonstrating representation in play
	BEING WILLING TO HAVE A GO ■ Initiating activities ■ Seeking challenge ■ Showing a 'can do' attitude ■ Taking a risk, engaging in new experiences, and learning by trial and error	I enjoy taking a risk, trying new things and learning by trial and error. I like to show a 'can do' attitude. I will seek out things that will challenge me. I can initiate activities.	■ Always ready to explore new experiences presented to them ■ Responds to provocations. (These will be explored in Chapter 3) ■ Demonstrates persistence, overcomes difficulties

	Learning opportunity	For the child	Examples
ACTIVE LEARNING - Motivation	**BEING INVOLVED AND CONCENTRATING** ■ Maintain focus on their activity for a period of time ■ Showing high levels of energy, fascination ■ Not easily distracted ■ Paying attention to details	I can keep focused on my activity, sometimes for a lengthy period of time. I exert energy and am fascinated by my task. I am totally absorbed and fully involved in my task.	Look out for the child who is fully engrossed in their task and remains involved for much longer than you would anticipate. They ignore any distractions around them as they are lost in the world of what they are doing.
	KEEP ON TRYING ■ Persisting with activity when challenges occur ■ Showing a belief that more effort or a different approach will pay off ■ Bouncing back after difficulties	I stick with an activity even when challenges arise. I am not deterred. I am able to bounce back after difficulties and persist. I believe that if I keep trying or change what I am doing, it will pay off.	The earlier example of the child described using the building blocks on page 7. Perfectly illustrates this characteristic.
	ENJOYING AND ACHIEVING WHAT THEY SET OUT TO DO ■ Showing satisfaction in meeting their own goals ■ Being proud of how they accomplished something – not just the end result ■ Enjoying meeting challenges for their own sake rather than external rewards or praise	I am really pleased when I meet my own goals and want to share my achievement. I am proud of what I have accomplished including the process, how I reached my goal. I get satisfaction from meeting challenges for myself and don't necessarily need external praise.	The baby who enjoys building up a couple of blocks and then knocking them down and laughs. The child described in the water play example on page 7 shows a child who is gaining satisfaction from meeting a challenge they set.

	Learning opportunity	For the child	Examples
CREATING AND THINKING CRITICALLY - Thinking	**HAVING THEIR OWN IDEAS** ■ Thinking of ideas ■ Finding ways to solve problems ■ Finding new ways to do things	I can develop my own ideas and make plans and follow through in my play. I will work to solve problems to enable my plan. I am able to find new ways to do things, making discoveries.	A child is engrossed in play with the trains on a table top with sand in the carriages. He creates a bridge for his track by pulling the tables apart. The bridge was needed for the narrative in his head of the story/plan he was following through.
	MAKING LINKS ■ Making links and noticing patterns in their experience ■ Making predictions ■ Testing their ideas ■ Developing ideas of grouping, sequences, cause and effect	I test out my ideas and discoveries to see if they are secure. I am able to make predictions about what I think will happen. I can connect experiences together noticing link and patterns between current and previous experiences.	■ Building sandcastles ■ Building a tall tower, is it secure? ■ Skilfully doing jigsaw puzzles ■ Exploring the properties of paint and using it in different ways ■ Cooking activity ■ Cause and effect toy e.g. a push and pop up toy
	ENJOYING AND ACHIEVING WHAT THEY SET OUT TO DO ■ Showing satisfaction in meeting their own goals ■ Being proud of how they accomplished something – not just the end result ■ Enjoying meeting challenges for their own sake rather than external rewards or praise	I am really pleased when I meet my own goals and want to share my achievement. I am proud of what I have accomplished including the process, how I reached my goal. I get satisfaction from meeting challenges for myself and don't necessarily need external praise.	■ Junk modelling ■ Small world play ■ Riding a tricycle ■ Role play ■ Play with non specific play materials ■ Colour mixing paint ■ Making play dough

How do children learn?

Reflection on how children learn as previously mentioned enables our teaching to be more effective and supportive of the learning process, so we are considerate to the child's needs, ensuring we are not invasive or controlling in our approach. Children need to be able to access all these methods of learning daily, as different children learn in different combinations of styles every day:

■ Through play

■ When experiences are in a meaningful context

■ Exploring, investigating and experimenting

■ By trial and error

■ Physical and intellectual challenge

■ Through repetition

■ First hand experiences, by doing

■ Communication with others or by talking to themselves

■ Modelling, being shown how to do something

■ By being with others

■ Direct and indirect teaching

■ Observing and imitating others

■ Seeking information from adults, peers or other sources

■ Problem solving

■ Applying what has been previously learnt

■ Evaluating what they have achieved.

The above are facilitated through play, child initiated activity and adult led activities.

Play, child initiated activity and adult led activities can be defined as follows:

Play is freely chosen by the child, and is under the control of the child. The child decides how to play, how long to sustain the play, what the play is about, and who to play with. There are many forms of play, but it is usually highly creative, open-ended and imaginative. It requires active engagement of the players, and can be deeply satisfying.

Child initiated activity has many characteristics in common with play, as it is wholly decided upon by the child, based on the child's own motivation, and remains under the child's control. It may involve play of many types, or it may be seen by the child as an activity with a serious purpose to explore a project or express an idea which the child may not see as pure play. It is guided by certain expectations within an early years setting regarding responsible use of space, time and purposes.

Adult led activities are those which adults initiate. The activities are not play, and children are likely not to see them as play, but they should be playful – with activities presented to children which are as open-ended as possible, with elements of imagination and active exploration that will increase the interest and motivation for children. As well as focused activities with groups of children, adult-led activities can include greeting times, story times, songs and even tidying up.

Learning, Playing and Interacting DCSF 2009

Play, as we know, is what enables key learning experiences for children, and as Froebel said 'play is a child's work' it is what they do. Play is how children make sense of the world, by reliving and recreating experiences and exploring ideas.

It is about their own interpretations, developing understanding and awareness. For this to happen to the optimum advantage, children need plenty of time to wallow in their play, be it alone or with others. Play is not only about resources with a specific purpose e.g. jigsaw, shape sorter, but also those which can be anything within the child's imagination e.g. an empty cardboard box, the carpet inner tube, the silk scarf. Play is the child's outlet, their expression of thoughts, feelings, ideas and curiosity.

Statements about play

Play is essential for children, it is what they do, how they discover about the world and themselves. As practitioners, it is important to reflect on just how and why play is so important:

- It is spontaneous although it may be stimulated by an adult

- It comes from the child's own intrinsic motivation

- It usually concentrates on a process not a product

- It has no explicit rules and no right or wrong way of performing

- It is an activity where children have ownership of what takes place

- The child is a willing and active participant

- it builds on the child's first hand experiences'

- Play is sometimes thought of as the opposite of work, as an amusement and a waste of time

- It is vital for children to have plenty of opportunity for free play, to enable them to develop fully, in an all round way

- It is an important part of education, through playing the child learns about herself, about other people and about the world in which she lives

- Play encourages the imagination and allows the child to experiment

- Play teaches social co-operation

- Play is an outlet for emotional development, the child can act out fears and worries

- Play aids physical development, it helps the child to gain control over his body and improve co-ordination

- The child needs to play freely but with a background of rules

- An important aspect of play is the interest it has for the child, he plays because he enjoys it

- Play is an end in itself, it does not necessarily have goals.

The facilitation of this learning is further explored in Chapter 3, The Physical Environment by identifying how the provision of play supports learning.

Thoughts on continuous provision

For quality teaching and learning to occur we want children to be fully involved and engaged. This is enabled through 'continuous provision' and the support we may give to children to extend learning, and create learning opportunities through planned adult led experiences. An adult led experience though needs to be presented with an element of freedom. The reflective question asked in the characteristics of effective learning should be considered each time we plan an activity:

'Is this an opportunity for children to find their own ways to represent and develop their own ideas?'

In essence, it is about us providing and then sitting back and seeing what happens and offering support and guidance if necessary. We are facilitators who need to enable children to wallow in an idea and explore their own interpretation.

Essentially we are merely onlookers, observing and learning ourselves, facilitators of high level learning and deep involvement. This will only be achieved for the child if we understand clearly what is quality teaching and how children learn.

We need children to be physically, emotionally and intellectually involved in their learning and if we sat back and looked at each child in the room, could we say they were all engaged to a high level, are we meeting the learning needs of all children?

Prof Ferre Laevers explores indicators for involvement. Laevers says that first you need to look at well being, how is the child feeling, and are his emotional and physical needs being met. Unless they are met, involvement will be of a lower level and therefore so will learning. Then you can consider their learning and levels of involvement. Observation using these scales can be supportive of our effectiveness and useful during settling in periods and transitions.

The Leuven Scale of well being

Level	Well Being	Signals
1	Extremely Low	The child clearly shows signs of discomfort such as crying or screaming. They may look dejected, sad, frightened or angry. The child does not respond to the environment, avoids contact and is withdrawn. The child may behave aggressively, hurting him/herself or others.
2	Low	The posture, facial expression and actions indicate that the child does not feel at ease. However, the signals are less explicit than under level 1 or the sense of discomfort is not expressed the whole time.
3	Moderate	The child has a neutral posture. Facial expression and posture show little or no emotion. There are no signs indicating sadness or pleasure, comfort or discomfort.
4	High	The child shows obvious signs of satisfaction (as listed under level 5). However, these signals are not constantly present with the same intensity.
5	Extremely High	The child looks happy and cheerful, smiles, cries out with pleasure. They may be lively and full of energy. Actions can be spontaneous and expressive. The child may talk to him/herself, play with sounds, hum, sing. The child appears relaxed and does not show any signs of stress or tension. He /she is open and accessible to the environment. The child expresses self confidence and self assurance.

The Leuven Scale of involvement

Level	Involvement	Signals
1	Extremely Low	Activity is simple, repetitive and passive. The child seems absent and displays no energy. They may stare into space or look around to see what others are doing.
2	Low	Frequently interrupted activity. The child will be engaged in the activity for some of the time they are observed, but there will be moments of non-activity when they will stare into space, or be distracted by what is going on around.
3	Moderate	Mainly continuous activity. The child is busy with the activity but at a fairly routine level and there are few signs of real involvement. They make some progress with what they are doing but don't show much energy and concentration and can be easily distracted.
4	High	Continuous activity with intense moments. The child's activity has intense moments and at all times they seem involved. They are not easily distracted.
5	Extremely High	The child shows continuous and intense activity revealing the greatest involvement. They are concentrated, creative, energetic and persistent throughout nearly all the observed period.

To enable clearer awareness of the involvement scale, Laevers identified key signals for involvement. These key signals enable us to identify and reflect clearly on children's involvement.

The child involvement signals

Concentration
- Attention of the child is directed towards the activity

- Nothing can distract the child from deep concentration.

Energy
- The child invests much effort in the activity, is eager and stimulated and is clearly expounding energy in the activity

- Energy is often expressed by loud talking or pressing down hard on paper

- Facial expression can reveal 'hard' thinking, e.g. a slight frown, tongue slightly poking out.

Complexity and creativity
The child is thinking and problem solving and is operating at a high level, at the edge of their capabilities.

Facial expression and posture
A facial expression can reveal intense concentration and, especially when seen from behind, a child's posture can reveal concentration or boredom. Posture demonstrating concentration might be rigid shoulders, hunched over.

Persistence
The duration of the concentration of an activity. Children who are really involved do not let an activity go easily, they want to continue.

Precision
Involved children show special care for their work and are attentive to detail.

Reaction time
Children who are involved are alert and react quickly to stimuli introduced during an activity.

Language
Children can show by their comments that an activity is important to them.

Satisfaction
Children display a feeling of satisfaction with their achievements.

These high levels of involvement are only going to occur if we have got the learning opportunities right for the child. The signals as indicators for involvement are 'observer

awareness' and should be used to build up a picture of the child's overall involvement. The signals can be displayed in different ways by different children. Having ascertained if a child is deeply involved we can then look more critically for a deeper analysis, considering what is about the experience/opportunity that has enabled this level of involvement? What can we learn about the child or the provision? How can we use this knowledge to further develop learning for the child?

The key reflective questions below sum up quality teaching, considering what more we can do and how we can move the child forward? We look at needs and interests and development levels, put it together and make informed decisions about exactly what it is that a child needs.

Individually, for key children we can consider the following:

- Where is the child at the moment developmentally?

- What is their preferred method of communication?

- What are their particular interests and likes?

- How do you use their likes and interests to support their learning?

Considering a child's interest is not saying, construction, but what is it within that play that the child explores, repeats and enjoys? To be effective we can't just look at the surface but need to delve deeper to understand what motivates the child to learn. It might be that the child is demonstrating/following a schema (see Chapter 4)

In conclusion quality teaching is about:

- Valuing each child

- Respecting what each individual can do

- Establish an ethos of trust through positive and purposeful interactions

- Build on successful learning experiences

- Encourage children to feel good about themselves

- Encouraging each child to try out new ideas

- Allow each child to express their feelings

- Encouraging each child to take risks

- Develop high self esteem and confidence in attempting new tasks

- Enable each child to explore and experiment with confidence

- Empower children to become autonomous learners

- Plan opportunities and time for children to pursue ideas and refine skills

- Show trust and give freedom for children to practice and consolidate

- Enable children to become independent researchers and investigators

- Plan opportunities for genuine collaborative learning

- Provide situations where children can learn from each other and develop mutual respect

- Develop effective working relationships

- Appreciate strengths and weaknesses.

The language of teaching

Effective use of language

How we use language is a key element of teaching and learning. It is about achieving a balance, not a constant barrage of language, but language used in thoughtful and considerate ways, whilst recognising the importance of silence and saying nothing.

Children do not need to experience a constant onslaught of inane questions, e.g. 'what colour is that', the child knows you are merely testing them, knows you know the answer, the child is probably thinking why am I being asked that? This type of question serves no purpose and often just interrupts the child's flow of thinking and is pointless. So, how should language be used as an effective support to teaching?

■ For the youngest children use simple language, reflecting their use of telegraphic speech and use single words in context, as they are quick to process and understand

■ Remember if you ask a child a valid question, they need time to process. First recognising they have been asked a question, then considering the response to the question and finally putting the words together to be able to answer it.

■ Use gestures and body language to support use of language for the youngest children and those with EAL

■ Consider the use of statements, which can be supportive of what a child is doing and can also be provocative, and supportive of critical thinking and analysis

■ Remember less is more and children often need silence and relative peace to process their thinking and ideas and do not want to be interrupted by questions or suggestions from an adult

■ Use language to remind children of what they have done before, to support them making links.

The ability to explore and use language opens up a whole new world to children enabling expression of thoughts, feelings and ideas. We need to provide ample opportunities and time for children to explore and experiment with language in their play and specific planned experiences. Equally we need to reflect on the types of language we use to broaden their understanding and vocabulary.

Definitions of language

1. **Speech:** an organised set of sounds which make up words. Sometimes we talk about articulation.

2. **Expressive language:** This is using words and sentences to communicate our feelings and ideas.

3. **Receptive language:** We use this term to describe listening and understanding what is said to us.

4. **Non-verbal language:** This is where we use gestures/facial expression, body language to communicate. In children non-verbal communication is seen in their play and social interactions.

Language and play dough

A group of pre school children are with a practitioner making play dough.

P: 'what have we used so far?'
CH: ' flour, salt, powder paint, oil'
P: 'what is missing?'
CH: 'water'
P: 'Jack can you go and fill this up to half way'.

Jack goes off with a jug and returns...

J: 'is this half full'
C2: 'no'
P: 'is it in the middle?'
J: 'yes'
P: 'not too near the top, not too near the bottom, so it is half full as it is in the middle'.

There are different types of language we can use for children at different development stages and circumstances to be supportive of learning.

Considering these types of language helps to reflect on what we say and how we can best support language appropriately for the individual child. It is easy to forget just how significant the way we say something can be for a child as they develop their language skills.

Helping children to talk

Self-talk

Here the adult is labelling what they are doing, describing and demonstrating and talking in the context of an activity, e.g. "I'm changing your nappy."

This enables children to make connections between words and actions, labelling in their minds and as these words are repeated to them, the understanding and word definition becomes secure. In the example given to consolidate understanding the practitioner needs to reinforce the word nappy, showing the child, so they can make a clear and specific link.

Parallel talk

In parallel talk you describe what the child is doing. As you interact with the child you comment on where the child is playing, what the child is playing with and possibly what the child is doing.

This doesn't mean a running commentary, but carefully considered language to identify key elements of what the child is doing e.g. actions or naming an object. There needs to be silence and pauses between what the adult says to enable the child to process and assimilate. The child may then repeat words that the adult has said, or simply just store away the vocabulary to build on at a later time.

Repeat

After listening carefully to a child, you repeat what the child has said. Repeating is effective because it clarifies what the child has said, serves as an acknowledgement, is very supportive of the language/words the child uses, and often keeps children talking because it acts like a question and indicates that you're interested in what they have to say. Repeat can also be useful when you are not absolutely sure what a child has said, by repeating you are clarifying if you have understood.

Restate

Sometimes children make mistakes when communicating. When a child makes a language error, you can repeat what they said in the correct form without drawing attention to the error. You are modelling correct language in a positive manner that helps communication and is supportive of grammatically correct language. The child can then reflect and process your use of language, as part of their evolving understanding.

Expanding

This is responding to a child, by saying something to expand and develop their thinking. A child might comment about what they are doing e.g. 'I'm building a castle' and the practitioner responds 'a castle, I wonder what your castle will look like when it is finished?' This can then perhaps get the child to consider and think about the process of building their castle, their plan and how they will know when it is finished.

Encouraging ideas

Encourage children to articulate their solutions and ideas by asking them how they solved something: by describing what they will do and what they did; and by asking them to help you. The last strategy is particularly valuable because it indicates your respect for their ideas and solutions to problems. 'How can I...', 'How can you...', 'What did you...?'

Open-ended questions

Questions that have more than one right answer, or ones that can be answered in many ways are called 'open-ended' or 'divergent' questions. These questions stimulate more language, respect the diversity of solutions, affirm children's ideas, support independence and encourage creative thinking. 'How can we make pink paint?', 'What do you need to play in the water?', 'How many more do we need?', 'What happened to...'.

Case study Encouraging language

After a painting activity a practitioner is helping a child of 16 months to get dressed. She shows the child the pile of clothes 'are these Emily's?' The child nods and the practitioner responds, 'what do we put on first?' The child takes her socks out of her shoes and gives them to the practitioner, she puts them on. The practitioner holds up her dress, 'is this Emily's dress?' The child nods and then first the practitioner puts on an all in one vest with poppers. The child says 'pop' and the adult repeats 'pop', as she closes the poppers. The practitioner then holds up the dress and says 'Emily's dress' and puts it on her. The practitioner says to the child, 'turn around so I can do up the button', she repeats turn around as she turns the child around.

Teaching, learning and language

The practitioner is engaging in conversation with the child using simple language. The questions used are easily understood and the practitioner responds to the non-verbal answers. The practitioner responds to the language the child uses 'by repeating' and she uses action to reinforce the term 'turn around'. This exchange is supportive of embedding key vocabulary, the child is a partner with the practitioner in the exchange and her contribution is valued.

Case study The power of silence

Teaching through modelling and silent support

Outside, three older babies are playing in the water tray. There are dolls in soapy water in the tray with very large spoons, flannels and sponges. The practitioner models using the spoons to scoop and dribble water over the dolls. Two children copy her actions, there is no language just silent support and modelling of repeated actions. One child scoops up some water and walks and pours it onto the garden, he returns to the water tray and continues to explore the soapy water using the large spoon and sponge. He then scoops up water and takes it and puts onto one of the plastic tricycles. He returns to the water tray and lifts a flannel out of the water and watches the water dripping from the flannel. The practitioner says to him 'it is dripping'.

Learning taking place

The practitioner did not bombard the children with language and questions, but gave them the space to make their own discoveries. She modelled an action which was copied by the children and one child extended further by transporting the water and dribbling in other places. Observing the child's fascination with the dripping water, the practitioner used language in that instance to give a name to what the child was watching.

Children need the space to think and process their observations, to enable connections and links to be made in their brains, and information to be stored. This was enabled by the practitioner in this scenario as, by remaining mostly silent, she was giving the children that space and time.

Effective use of language

It is often just as important to consider the 'how not' as well as the 'how to', concerning language and children. Show how to use language supportively.

Supportive use of language	Ineffective use of language
In a 2-3 year old room of a day nursery a practitioner is playing a picture match lotto game with a group of four of the older children. As each child selects their card, she prompts them asking if it is one of theirs. Leaving time for a response, then carefully asks simple questions about what is in the picture, again with pauses. The practitioner is using simple language, reinforcing the children's understanding and giving them time to respond.	In a pre school room a child is deeply involved with play with zoo animals in a tuff spot with shredded paper. She has a clear narrative in her head and is using language to tell her story as she moves the animals around. A practitioner approaches the child and points to the animal she is holding and asks her 'what animal is that?' The practitioner took no time to ascertain and observe what the child was doing, but simply approached and used language in an inane way and interrupted the child's thought processes.
Exchange between a practitioner and two children in a pre school: **P:** 'how many pieces of cereal are in the bowl?' **C:** '64' **P:** 'That is a very good estimate' **P to C2:** 'how many pieces of cereal are in the bowl?' **C2:** '4' **P:** 'We can count 4' They count the four pieces of cereal in the bowl **P:** 'There are a lot more than four' This exchange is an example of mathematical vocabulary being used in a context children can understand, with the use of 'estimate' and 'more than'. Whilst the children may not have understood completely what estimate means, vocabulary has to be used in a context so that over time, they understand the meaning.	
In a pre school, children explore construction and the adult uses mathematical vocabulary in context, 'put one this side to balance', 'it is too small', 'yes you need a bigger one', 'what would make it steadier?', 'a flatter surface means more to balance on' As the language was being used in an appropriate context, the children would be able to associate the words with the actions and maybe go on to use these themselves.	
Exchange between a practitioner and a children in a pre school: **P:** 'What do you like on your crackers that we haven't had today?' **C:** 'honey, I have honey on my crackers at home' **P:** 'You have honey on your crackers at home. I have marmite on my crackers at home.' The children were having crackers for tea with a choice of toppings. The practitioner asked an open-ended question to extend thought and make connections. She then repeated the child's response to affirm and show value to what was said and added additional information.	

Case study Language at story time

A practitioner is reading a story to a group of pre school children. The children are listening with rapt attention and respond to elements of the story with 'huh', 'ouch'. The practitioner puts emphasis on key words/phrases in the story, e.g. 'bright green' and the children spontaneously repeat phrases from the story 'uh oh', indicating involvement and enjoyment. At points she waits for the children fill in with what is next: P 'and' Children 'abracadabra'. The practitioner also uses facial expression to help convey the story.

Learning to have fun with language and enjoy the sounds of language from enthusiastic practitioners is essential. It encourages children to be curious and want to explore and experiment with language.

The use of statements

As previously mentioned, the use of statements can be an extremely effective language tool. Statements give the child the choice as to whether or not they wish to respond. At the same time they acknowledge what the child is doing and if used appropriately and sparingly they can be supportive of learning and act as a stimulus to thought and ideas. Statements require some reflection and thinking and aren't as easy to think of as questions. Here are some examples.

Activity	Example statements
A cooking activity	'The sugar has disappeared into the butter.' 'The flour is floating into the bowl.' 'You are mixing all the ingredients.'
A collage activity	'You have made a pattern.' 'You are sticking very carefully.' 'Glue sticks things.'
Looking at plants that have grown	'They look different' 'They have grown'
Painting	'Swirls of colours' 'The colours are merging'
Den building outside	'This is a secure structure.' 'It looks cosy.' 'Your idea has worked.'
Looking at a picture or non fiction book together	'Oh' 'Interesting' 'I can see so much'

The key is variety, using language to match the situation and the development stage of the child. What will work best here? Should I use language or would it be better to remain silent? How can I use language to support acquisition? How can I use language to develop learning and extend thought? How do you adapt your language to meet the children's needs?

It is easy to get into a rut or a habit in relation to the language we use with children.

Characteristics of effective learning

These reflective practice questions from the positive relationships descriptor of the Characteristics of Effective Learning in *Development Matters*, can help us to consider carefully our use of language and its breadth.

Playing and exploring:
What adults can do (positive relationships)

- Play with children. Encourage them to explore, and show your own interest in discovering new things. Ensuring we do not take over by directing and over talking but allowing the children to guide the play and interact from their lead

- Help children as needed to do what they are trying to do, without taking over or directing. Give careful and considered suggestion for the child to contemplate

- Join in play sensitively, fitting in with children's ideas. Join in if they invite, ensuring they take the lead and that you are merely a participant

- Model pretending an object is something else, and help develop roles and stories. This can be done through mimicking, using an object to represent something using appropriate language, especially with the youngest children. The development of roles and stories can be through discussion and the use of props

- Encourage children to try new activities and to judge risks for themselves. Be sure to support children's confidence with words and body language. Be an onlooker, providing support and minimal words as necessary, so the child can think and reflect

- Pay attention to how children engage in activities, - the challenges faced, the effort, thought, learning and enjoyment. Talk more about the process than the product. Observe and then discuss and comment on what they did and their choices

- Talk about how you and the children get better at things through effort and practice, and what we all can learn when things go wrong.

Active Learning:
What adults can do (positive relationships)

- Support children to choose their activities – what they want to do and how they will do it. Remind them of what they have done before, enable choice, encourage them to consider how they might do something

- Stimulate children's interest through shared attention, and calm over-stimulated children. Demonstrate an interest in what the child enjoys and likes

- Help children to become aware of their own goals, make plans, and review their own progress. Describe what you see them trying to do, and encourage children to talk about their own successes. This might begin with parallel talk for the younger children, progressing to discussion and reflection, through carefully considered questions

- Be specific when you praise, especially noting effort, such as how the child concentrates, tries different approaches, persists, solves problems, and has new ideas

- Encourage children to learn together and from each other.

- Set up opportunities for collaborative work together and support children as they move through the social stages of development in play, particularly from solitary play, to parallel, to associative

- Children develop their own motivations when you give reasons and talk about learning, rather than just directing. Discuss processes and set challenges.

Creating and thinking critically:
What adults can do (positive relationships)

- Use the language of 'thinking and learning': think, know, remember, forget, idea, makes sense, plan, learn, find out, confused, figure out, trying to do. Use these words in an appropriate context so the children begin to understand their meaning and eventually use them

- Model being a thinker, showing that you don't always know, are curious and sometimes puzzled, and can think and find out, use words such as 'I wonder', 'perhaps', 'maybe'

- Encourage open-ended thinking by not settling on the first ideas: What else is possible?

- Always respect children's efforts and ideas, so they feel safe to take a risk with a new idea

- Talking aloud helps children to think and control what they do. Model self-talk, describing your actions in play

- Give children time to talk and think. Valuing silence and thought, watch for children thinking

- Value questions, talk and consider many possible responses, without rushing toward answers too quickly. Children need to ponder and reflect before replying

- Support children's interests over time, reminding them of previous approaches and encouraging them to make connections between their experiences

- Model the creative process, showing your thinking about some of the many possible ways forward. 'We could do this, or maybe we could...'

- Sustained shared thinking helps children to explore ideas and make links. Follow children's lead in conversation, and think about things together

- Encourage children to describe problems they encounter, and to suggest ways to solve the problem. 'Why do you think that happened?' 'What could we do to solve the problem?'

- Show and talk about strategies – how to do things – including problem-solving, thinking and learning

- Give feedback and help children to review their own progress and learning. Talk with children about what they are doing, how they plan to do it, what worked well and what they would change next time

- Model the plan-do-review process yourself. Discuss with the children why you have decided to do an activity and afterwards chat about how you and they feel it went.

As well as what we say or don't say, we need to ensure that the environment is supportive of language so there is a stimulus for us and the children. Curiosity and inquisitiveness can draw out language, acting as a stimulus, bring about a verbal response.

Non-verbal communication

The ability to be able to communicate with children non verbally and to read and understand their non verbal communications is essential. This demonstrates the practitioners ability to understand the child and tune into their thinking. When vocabulary is limited for whatever reason, it is supportive and encourages communication. If we ignore or fail to recognise non verbal communication, we are not only missing potential learning opportunities, but also the recognition of children's attempts at communication.

Supporting communication and language – enabling environments

The table below explores the suggestions from *Development Matters* on how to provide an environment that supports childrens communication and language.

Suggestion	Examples
Collect resources that children can listen to and learn to distinguish between.	■ Shells ■ Items that rattle ■ Sound lotto ■ Musical instruments ■ Recordings of the voices of different practitioners and/or children to listen to can be a fun activity
Encourage children to learn one another's names and to pronounce them correctly.	Photographs can facilitate this during a circle time/small group discussion. Children helping to put out placemats at lunch time.
Help children be aware of different voice sounds by using a mirror to see what their mouth and tongue do as they make different sounds.	Use wall mirrors (for babies) and hand held mirrors. Together, look at the shape your mouths make for different sounds and words.
Use actions and props with stories and rhymes.	Props, with stories and rhymes, enable involvement and support children to remember the narrative. Story props made available to children to retell a story for themselves is particularly supportive of language.
Provide resources that prompt interest and curiosity and stimulate language.	Simple every day objects can be perfect, the every day to us is curious to a child. This is particularly true of items they may see adults using and never get to use themselves. This type of exploration will stimulate language and is a great opportunity for the practitioner and child to discuss together.
Set up displays reminding children of what they have experienced.	The use of photos can facilitate this and stimulate discussion. Memory recall is supportive of the process of acquiring language.
Provide practical experiences that encourage children to ask and respond to questions.	The more innovative and exciting the activities, the better the opportunities for language
Provide fiction and non fiction books for children.	Each type of book provides a different language stimulus and can be used effectively for teaching in different ways.
Use lots of signs in the setting, both indoors and outdoors, to create a literacy rich environment.	Signs can provide a stimulus for conversation and discussion, particularly those that indicate how many children can play in a particular area or those which ask children to identify if they have played in a particular area.

Language is one of the keys to learning. It is through language that we can gain an insight into children's thinking, and we can use language carefully to extend learning and provoke thought and ideas. Children need adults who will:

■ Support emerging language by listening and responding, including imitating and repeating sounds for babies

■ Use language in a variety of ways, not just for asking questions or requesting co-operation, but to plan, recall, imagine, invent, consider, speculate and to share jokes

■ Value their non verbal communication and understand the importance of gestures to support spoken language

■ Encourage conversation

■ Observe children carefully to know when and how to introduce new vocabulary most effectively so they can understand the meaning and context of it

■ Understand the stages and processes of language development

■ Respect the need for silence.

Language needs to be respected and understood as a powerful tool in the process of learning.

By valuing children's language and being supportive of the process of its acquisition, we are enabling children to associate language with learning, while being respectful of that process.

Case study Use of verbal and non-verbal communication in a painting activity

In a toddler room of a day nursery, 4 children aged between 16 months and 2 years, are accessing a painting activity. The children have access to sponge dabbers, small paint pots (which just fit the sponge dabbers, so a challenge for the children), paint brushes, glue spreaders and their hands, they are painting on paper plates, doilies and onto the table.

The practitioner says the name of the colour, just the single word as the child uses it. A child is using the tools, saying with pleasure 'waa waa', the practitioner repeats 'waa, waa, you enjoying that Alice!'

The children are all engrossed and involved in the activity, exploring the paint and making marks, the practitioner offers support as necessary. One child takes a paint pot to try and print with and then uses his finger. He looks around and the practitioner asks, 'more paint?' and he nods in response. The practitioner gets the bottle of paint and says to the child ' can you help...and squeeze' he responds and puts his hands on the bottle.

A practitioner says to another child 'mix it', which is repeated by the child. 'You did it, good girl!' says the practitioner, and the child repeats 'did it'.

A child tries to put his hand in the paint pot, he stops and then says 'more' the practitioner responds by getting more paint.

What the practitioner said

The activity was set up as the children in the room love painting, it is provided most days and if it isn't out, the children will go to the cupboard where the paint is kept and rattle the door, clear expression of interest and choice.

What learning took place and why

The children were able to access the activity in their own way using the tools as they wished, exploring the use of the tools in the paint. The emphasis was on the process and the sensory experience, promoting expression and independence. The practitioner supported the children effectively responding to their verbal and non-verbal requests and using language appropriately.

Case study Using language to support scissors skills

A child in a pre school is at the mark making table and decides she wishes to cut paper. The practitioner asks her which hand she uses when she writes, the child holds up her right hand. The practitioner says 'that is your right hand, so you need a red pair of scissors.'

The child picks up a red pair of scissors and the practitioner guides her to put her 'thumb in here and three fingers in there'. The practitioner holds the paper taut for the child to cut, the practitioner encourages the child to repeat 'open and shut'. As the cutting progresses she remarks 'you are cutting Francesca'. The child cuts across the paper and the practitioner says 'good girl you did it, you went all the way through'.

The child then holds a piece of paper herself to cut, the practitioner continues to encourage 'open and shut... you've got it well done...can she make it across...there she goes, well done.'

The child then continues cutting by herself independently with no practitioner support, as she is now confident in her skills and abilities, she takes a piece of card and is able to cut through it.

Why this is effective use of language

The practitioner isn't using language incessantly but for a purpose to encourage and praise. The simple use of 'open and shut', is almost like a rhythmic pattern to help the child with the scissor cutting action. It is repeated a few times with pauses, so as not to overload the child. The practitioner uses parallel talk and statements to label what the child is doing and to offer encouragement 'you are cutting', continuing with 'you went all the way through'. At the end she affirms to the child saying 'you've got it well done.'

This kind of gentle support and use of affirmative language, is effective as it doesn't require a verbal response from the child, but acknowledges effort, process and achievement.

Questions to support learning and challenge with construction play

Measurement

If both buildings have the same number of blocks, what makes this one taller?

How can we find out which building has more blocks?

Shapes/Patterns

Describe the shape

How do we know it is a ... (circle, square, etc.)?

If we turn the shape upside down/sideways what happens to the shape?

How can we estimate/guess the number of blocks used?

What do you think is similar to this structure (or shape)?

How can you use the blocks to make one big _____ ?

How can you extend this into a pattern?

Balance

Why doesn't your tower fall down?

How can we use these blocks to make something really tall that doesn't fall down?

How can we use these blocks to make something that is really long?

How can you make a bridge that goes over part of the structure?

Concepts of ramps

Which container moves down the ramp fastest/slowest?

What is same/different?

What doesn't move and why?

How can you change the _____ to have it move faster?

What can you add to the ramp to slow down the movement?

What angle of the ramp makes it go faster/slower?

The building

How can you make sure _____ (animal etc) doesn't escape?

What will the people do in your building?

What happens when it rains on your house/the castle/the hotel etc.? What can you do to help the people inside stay dry?

What do the people need inside of the _____, outside of the _____ ?

How can you build those items?

The physical environment

The physical or learning environment is basically the blank canvas that you begin with and you fill with appropriate and stimulating experiences for the children. It is the tool for learning and creates opportunities for you to support that learning; the quality of your teaching can in some instances be directly related to the quality of the environment. As Maria Montessori said 'the goal of early childhood education should be to activate the child's own natural desire to learn.' That should be the aim of what you want your learning environment to achieve and enable.

An effective learning environment is about having a broad range of resources, carefully planned and organised areas and supportive and informed practitioners. However, you might have the most amazingly resourced environment, but it is the adults who make the difference. This applies to both the indoor and outdoor environment.

When planning the learning environment, we need to consider the following, ensuring we are providing experiences that:

- Allow children to feel happy, secure and comfortable

- Meet individual needs suited to learning requirements

- Reflect each child's social and cultural background

- Reflect the languages used by the children

- Value and build on previous experiences, the starting point is always where children are at, supported by the continuous provision

- Involve parents

- Are accessible and open-ended the emphasis on the process and not the end product, enabling children to develop ideas and their thinking to flow as they play and learn

- Give opportunity for first hand experiences, children learn by doing

- Give children the freedom and space to explore, allow flexibility and give time

- Develop confidence and self esteem through achievable challenges

- Allow time for children to assimilate their experiences

- Promote independence and autonomy making choices and decisions

- Allow for continuity of play

- Allow for a variety of learning situations

- Encourage the development of skills and attitudes

- Foster social relationships be reflective of the social stages of development in play

- Encourage communication

- Allow the child time for solitary activity respecting the ways in which children learn

- Develop positive attitudes to learning through self initiated activity and decision making

- Motivate the child to learn

- Allow for the development of the process skills involved in experiential learning.

You also need to consider and reflect on key conflicts within the environment, to ensure it is delivering what it needs to for the children:

- Choice vs control

- Exploration vs closed experiences

- Broadened experiences or stifled opportunities?

What is happening in your environment, how and why? It is essential that choice is enabled and not limited, even if that choice is just between two resources in an area or a baby leaning towards one floor toy as opposed to another: it is still about 'choice'. By enabling choice you learn about the child, whereas if everything is controlled by the adult, he gains no insight, the child's learning suffers and is not expanded, but very narrow. We need to constantly be striving to make discoveries about the children.

Choice then enables exploration and exploration supports learning and discovery. Exploration could be digging

outside and moving mud around, or discovering cornflour or following through an idea in play involving construction and dressing. Exploration breeds ideas and discovery, it enables a wealth of experiences for the child, building up their knowledge. If everything within the environment is carefully contained and freedom to explore is not enabled then opportunities, and in turn learning, become stifled.

To enable this discovery and broadening of experience, the environment needs to be organised into 'areas of experience', what these areas are will depend on the age and stage of development of the children. There will be differences between a baby room which needs to have cosy corners and plenty of floor space, to a pre school room or reception class, which will have clearly defined areas of learning and aspects of play.

For the areas of experience to work in any room, you should:

- Regularly review provision and revise in response to children's needs

- Have clear aims and objectives that are understood by all adults

- Use materials and equipment that are of a high standard, clean and safe; well structured equipment that is open-ended and allows for child initiated experiences

- Create visually defined boundaries for each area of experience, through use of carpets, furniture, storage units

- Keep equipment well maintained in a variety of storage e.g. silhouettes for matching 2D and 3D, in baskets, storage jars, in open shelf units, all clearly labelled, numbered parking bays for bikes outside

- Have available all the necessary equipment to ensure that the areas are self contained

- Use equipment that encourages play at all levels and caters for the differing stages of development

- Give opportunities for children to take resources from other areas to develop play and combine different equipment

- Consider additional equipment/materials to enhance play when appropriate, to initiate interest and follow up a child's idea.

What is provided within the environment directly impacts on the quality of children's experiences and it is worth considering these reflective practice questions when reviewing the environment and the children's learning needs:

■ What are the children currently interested in doing?

■ What skills are they developing?

■ How much space do you have available for different areas?

■ What other resources could you make available?

■ Are the children aware that there are other resources they can use to enhance their choices?

However, of equal benefit can be looking at the environment, particularly the outdoor environment, from a different perspective.

These prompts from Learning through Landscapes Cymru (First Steps Outdoors) provide some differing ideas for reflecting on provision outside, but equally most could be considered for inside. How do you provide these experiences and opportunities for children?

Where can children:

■ Be excited, energetic, adventurous, noisy

■ Have responsibility, be independent

■ Imagine, dream, invent

■ Hide, relax, find calm, reflect

■ Investigate, discover, explore, experiment

■ Run, climb, pedal, throw

■ Talk, collaborate, make friends

■ Create, construct, make music, express

■ Dig, grow, nurture

■ Tell stories, make marks, find patterns.

Can you identify these opportunities within your learning environment?

The layout of the environment has a huge impact on learning as it influences how children move between experiences and their ability to access resources. The areas need to be carefully planned and organised.

Maria Montessori believed that order plays an important part in children's lives, and that order consists of recognising that there is a place for everything within that environment and remembering where that is, 'a place for everything and everything in its place'. Montessori believed that this order made children feel safe and secure and therefore was supportive of learning.

Part of the quality of the provision is about the organisation of, access to and standard of the resources. Clutter can confuse children and we can have too much red, yellow, blue and green plastic replicas, particularly in home corner provision. We may all have experienced the scenario where you open the 'washing machine' in the home corner and everything tumbles out. These plastic replicas are giving children a false impression; we certainly don't cook with plastic. It is much better to give children real everyday objects as this enhances the experience for them. They will know when they are using something that is the same or very similar to an item used at home. Curiosity and interest will be greatly increased with the use of real objects, as from the perspective of sensory development there is so much more for the children to experience. Resources need to be appropriate and accessible, clearly labelled, in good repair and well maintained. Resources and the learning environment are the key tools to unlocking learning for children and need to be given significant thought, planning and preparation.

Baby room		Toddler
■ Cosy corners ■ Mirrors ■ Messy play ■ Explorations	■ Natural materials ■ Light ■ Black, white and red areas ■ Ramps for crawling over	■ Space ■ Consider their need to deconstruct before they can construct ■ Time to develop independence ■ Home corner ■ Visual routine
Pre school		**Reception (plus what is applicable for pre school)**
■ Have you got too many tables, is there enough floor space? Remember children, especially boys find it easier to access experiences on the floor. It is about their gross motor skills and development of core muscles ■ Visual routine ■ Clearly defined areas ■ Self registration ■ Science/food technology area, with free access to child led recipes with containers of flour, salt, food colouring etc to make their own play dough. For science, access to cornflour, pipettes, blotting paper, inks etc. ■ Have mini me photos of the children to use in their small world play ■ Have 'what tidy looks like' photos.		■ Interactive areas ■ Clearly defined areas ■ Resources to support literacy and numeracy ■ 'Who has played here' signs, so the children can move their names on a chart ■ Written self registration ■ 'Question of the day' chart, that can used as a discussion. Children answer yes or no to a question and then in a later discussion have to put their reason into a sentence.

As part of this planning preparation, it is important to consider what might be the key elements of the environment for different age ranges, that support and impact on children's learning and development, as part of any review process.

What about your routine? The routine has a huge impact on children's capacity and opportunity to learn. Children need at least an hour and a half to become fully absorbed in play. This might not necessarily be with the same experience, but they need the time to find where they want to be to immerse and to wallow. A routine that stops and starts, interrupts the flow and reduces the opportunity for the children to be immersed in their learning. The key question has to be: is the routine meeting the needs of the children or the needs of the setting and/or the adults?

Key considerations about the routine

■ The less there is in the routine the better

■ If you have access from your indoor environment directly to the outdoor, children need to access it as soon as possible in the day

■ Some children need to get outside straightaway this can be particularly relevant for boys and two year olds. Remember boys are much more likely to learn outside than inside

■ Children need to be active, particularly in toddler and pre school rooms, they do not need to sit down as they

arrive for registration, they need to be doing. A daily repetitive group discussion about the weather and what is on offer serves no purpose. The children need to be outside, experiencing the weather, and moving around the environment finding out what is available. Generally, they will know what is in the continuous provision and perhaps already have an idea of what they wish to engage with

■ Do you have a snack time or a rolling snack? Snack time can take quite a chunk out of the day, especially if you tidy up beforehand. Rolling snack supported by an adult can give focus to supported learning and enable children to access as they wish and not interrupt their flow of learning. This is assuming an adult does not interrupt them telling them they need to have their snack

■ Transitions in the day need to be carefully managed. Are the children able to access the provision or is it packed away in anticipation of future events e.g. lunch

■ Ensure that in the routine, story time is not used as a filler, but as an exciting, stimulating and enjoyable learning experience, that is carefully planned

■ Is your routine about the children or the adults? Is it planned with the needs of the nursery in mind or the needs of the children?

■ Is your environment set up, so that as part of the routine children can look after their own needs e.g. put paintings to dry, wash hands, help themselves to water?

As you plan and review the environment you need to also take into account the facilitation of free flow play, which enables high level learning through child initiated experiences, as the children direct and follow through their own ideas and thoughts. Some practitioners may have concerns about children moving resources around, but they need to understand the importance and value of this. It is in free flow play that ideas emerge and grow.

Independence in the environment supported through the routine

At snack time, a child of 2 and a half collects her china plate and cup from a table and carries them to the snack table where she sits down. She then selects her snack choice and pours a drink from a small jug. Having finished the snack she carries the plate and cup to another table where a washing up bowl is situated, washes her plate and cup and then dries it.

Free flow play

Free flow play is when children can be fully absorbed in their play, moving from experience to experience. They use symbolic, manipulative, play with props, and physical play using their experience and ideas, allowing them to learn through discovery.

Free flow play was first described by Tina Bruce in 1991, this is a summary of the twelve features that characterise it:

1. it is an active process without a product
2. it is intrinsically motivated
3. there is no external pressure to conform
4. it is about lifting 'players' to their highest levels of functioning, involving creativity and imagination
5. it involves reflection, the wallowing of an idea
6. it actively uses previous first hand experience
7. it is sustained and helps us to function ahead of our real life ability levels
8. it allows control, using competence previously attained
9. it can be initiated by a child or an adult, but adults need to be aware of not imposing rules, or directing activity
10. it can be a solitary experience
11. it can be in partnership with others
12. it brings together what we learn, we feel and understand.

Tina Bruce, *Time to Play in Early Childhood Education* (1991), Hodder and Stoughton Ltd.

When presenting activities and experiences for children, we need to consider how this is done. Children, especially boys can find it hard to sit at a table from a physical development perspective, they may prefer to stand up or to access on the floor. Tables can be limiting in that there is only a limited number of them in a room, use of the floor can enable expansion and for children to lie down to access, which some will find easier. Consider what will work best for your children.

Observe to see which children particularly like the floor to play on. Give the children the option of standing at tables, observe to see who finds sitting on a chair and engaging in an activity particularly difficult. Do you need all of your tables? Can you remove some to create more space? If possible let the children choose between floor or table. Sometimes, children who do show a preference for a table, might access and engage in different ways, using different skills when an activity is on the floor.

Case study Free flow play in action

While observing in a pre school setting, I saw that the free flow play was particularly effective and strong. The children moved confidently and freely between experiences, both indoors and outdoors. Practitioners responded to the children moving around, to be with them as appropriate and responding to their needs and interests if necessary. There was a constant flow as children and adults were both engaged. The room had clearly defined areas, children played alone, associatively and in full cooperative play. Children problem solved, directed their own learning and were independent in terms of looking after their own needs and making choices and decisions. **The key factor is that the adults free flow as well as the children.**

The children were dressing up in clothes in different ways and used them in many aspects of play. During my observation, activities on a central carpet area flowed from a maths activity, to small world to a puppet show. Two girls walked around the setting carrying a plastic treasure chest, until they found the right spot for the role play they had in mind.

Snapshot

INSIDE
3 children listening to story with a practitioner
1 child mark making
5 children at the play dough table with a practitioner
3 children looking at caterpillars with a practitioner
2 children playing with magnetic Perspex shapes
4 children playing in their own devised role play
2 children at the computer

OUTSIDE
1 child on trampette
1 child on stepping stones
2 children by the tuff spot
2 practitioners

Why did it work?

Free flow play is about children being able to follow through their ideas and take the lead in their own learning, with the opportunity to be alone or with others, both adults and children. The adults need to be aware of all that is going on and support children if they become disengaged, or respond to their needs by extending the provision through additional resources and by being involved. Adults need to be sensitive, achieving a balance where they are not taking over but are enablers.

In this example, there was a seamless flow of movement, the children were permanently engaged, sometimes remaining for long periods of times at an experience, at times for a shorter period. They were confident and knew not only where resources were, but also that they could move them between areas, if needed for their play. Children moved from playing alone, to being with a group, sometimes with and sometimes without a practitioner.

Activities and experiences reflected children's interests and were clearly selected carefully with enhancements added to the continuous provision. Every child in that setting would have gained from access to the free flow play, as the levels of involvement were high.

The enabling environment

The characteristics of effective learning provide us with guidance to enable reflection on the enabling environment, and to consider if we are providing the best we can to support learning and meeting children's needs.

Playing and exploring	How	Ways to develop and improve
■ Provide stimulating resources which are accessible and open-ended so they can be used, moved and combined in a variety of ways. ■ Make sure resources are relevant to children's interests. ■ Arrange flexible indoor and outdoor space and resources where children can explore, build, move and role play. ■ Help children concentrate by limiting noise, and making spaces visually calm and orderly. ■ Plan first-hand experiences and challenges appropriate to the development of the children. ■ Ensure children have uninterrupted time to play and explore.	■ Choice ■ Accessible storage ■ Photos of resources not available ■ Free flow play ■ Ordered layout ■ Resources children enjoy, and tap into their natural curiosity ■ Interests board ■ Transportable resources e.g. carry boxes ■ Visually not too busy and overly bright ■ Enable exploration ■ Well planned ■ Routine that is supportive of wallowing in an idea.	
Active learning		
■ Children will become more deeply involved when you provide something that is new and unusual for them to explore, especially when it is linked to their interests. ■ Notice what arouses children's curiosity, looking for signs of deep involvement to identify learning that is intrinsically motivated. ■ Ensure children have time and freedom to become deeply involved in activities. ■ Children can maintain focus on things that interest them over a period of time. Help them to keep ideas in mind by talking over photographs of their previous activities. ■ Keep significant activities out instead of routinely tidying them away. ■ Make space and time for all children to contribute.	■ Use provocations ■ Reflect interest in planning ■ Observe carefully and reflect ■ Well planned routine meeting the needs of the children ■ Photos on the wall, in books, in learning journals ■ Continuous provision ■ Enable children to revisit planned adult led activities ■ Listen to children's suggestions and ideas and record.	
Creating and thinking critically		
■ In planning activities, ask yourself: is this an opportunity for children to find their own ways to represent and develop their own ideas? Avoid children just reproducing someone else's ideas. ■ Build in opportunities for children to play with materials before using them in planned tasks. ■ Play is a key opportunity for children to think creatively and flexibly, solve problems and link ideas. Establish the enabling conditions for rich play: space, time, flexible resources, choice, control, warm and supportive relationships. ■ Recognisable and predictable routines help children to predict and make connections in their experiences. ■ Routines can be flexible, while still basically orderly. ■ Plan linked experiences that follow the ideas children are really thinking about. ■ Use mind-maps to represent thinking together. ■ Develop a learning community which focuses on how and not just what we are learning.	■ Reflection on the process explore the properties and purpose of materials e.g. paint ■ Value play ■ Consistency ■ Observe, listen, reflect and plan ■ Share and discuss ideas.	

Case study Activities don't need to be on tables

Balance in an adult led activity

A group of four 2 year olds are engaged in an activity outside on the ground, with a practitioner. She tells them 'we are going to make a tall tower'. Each child is given a pot of glue with some paint, she tells them 'first we need to mix our glue'. They begin to mix and she says 'mix it up'. One child picks up a cereal box and looks inside and says 'empty', he then begins to smear his glue spreader over the box, each child takes a box and does the same. They carefully spread the glue over the boxes, the practitioner comments ' I like the strokes you are making', 'all over', 'more glue', lots of glue'. The children continue fascinated by the glue and encouraged by the practitioner. She asks a child 'are you going to do the other side?' 'turn it over'. The practitioner then demonstrates on one box pouring the glue onto the box and the children watch. One of the children copies her pouring glue onto his box and he then kneels up over his box and swirls and spreads the glue around with the glue spreader. The other children begin to balance and pile up their boxes, the practitioner says, 'put your box on top, and another box'. She then says 'look how tall it is, we will let it dry'.

Learning taking place

This was an adult led activity which enabled the children to explore the glue freely and to experiment. They had a large surface over which to spread the glue. The practitioner was there as a support and modelled the action of pouring the glue. All of the children were interested and engaged. This activity will also help them to understand the properties of glue, that you use glue for sticking. Additionally, as the activity was carried out on the ground, the children were able to access in a different way, especially the child who knelt up over his box.

A missed opportunity?

The tower was as tall as the boys were in height, so it would have been interesting for them to have had the opportunity to stand by their tower and compare.

Provocations

Part of the practitioner's role to support learning within the environment and create potential opportunities for effective teaching is the use of provocations. Provocations are designed to stimulate thoughts, ideas, discussion, questions, creativity and possibilities. They should be presented with no fanfare or introduction, just simply be there for the children to be curious about and want to explore. An effective provocation is an example of effective teaching, as you have tapped into the children's natural curiosity and made them want to explore further. As the explorations occur, you may ponder with the children, perhaps with the use of statements or further thoughts.

Here are some examples of provocations:

- Lay out a length of blue cellophane along the floor, placing pebbles along each side, a river or is it?

- Put herbs in the tuff spot with scissors

- Transient art with picture frames using single large beads, strings of beads and natural materials

- Roll a length of foil across the floor and place stones around the edge, what do the children do?

- Place into a pot labelled 'magic wands' sticks with ribbons attached

- Hole punch with leaves

- Weave wool across a large plastic hula hoop , so the children can then weave ribbon through the wool

- Freeze leaves and petals in ice cubes and put out with torches

- Ice and chalk in the tuff spot

- A collection of plumbing pipes and connectors in the middle of a construction area

- Clear away the tables, so the children just have use of the floor and other surfaces, how does this change what they do?

- Clear away resources as much as you can and provide the children with lots of cardboard boxes and masking tape

- Painting a real tree branch

- Wool or wire to wrap round large stones, what do the children do?

- Clearing out the role play area or home corner, so there are no resources, do the children create and find their own improvised resources?

Ofsted statement (good criteria)	What it means / what Ofsted will be looking for
Practitioners teach the basics well and support children to learn the communication and language skills and develop the physical, personal, social and emotional skills they need for the next steps in their learning. Where appropriate, early literacy skills and mathematical development are promoted effectively to ensure that children are ready for school.	Opportunities are used throughout the day to support learning in the prime areas. Particularly for the youngest children, there is a focus on the prime areas; this should be reflected both indoors and outdoors. There is evidence as appropriate of a literacy and numeracy rich environment, with interactive opportunities for children. Numbers are used in a context with meaning and mixed mark making opportunities are available, again inside and outside.
Practitioners provide a wide range of opportunities for children to learn about people and communities beyond their immediate experience. Resources and activities reflect and value the diversity of children's backgrounds and experiences.	If possible trips are made out into the local community and visitors are invited into the setting, who can share something of value with the children. The backgrounds of all the children are considered and reflected in displays, celebrations and resources available to the children. This is done though in a way which is meaningful for the children.

The environment should be a learning tool in itself, so the consideration we give to it is critical. We need to look at what is providing for the children, both as a whole and individually, reviewing regularly.

- Who plays in and accesses the different areas in the room? Are there areas some children never access?

- Are there any activities which are excluded to some groups of children or individuals who find an area difficult to access for some reason?

- When did each child face the challenge of something new?

- Do children actively seek help or information from adults?

- Do children respond well to the introduction of new resources?

- Is the environment supporting progress and learning? (link with assessment)

- Do you involve children in the planning of the environment?

Children's learning in many ways can only be as strong as the environment with which they interact. It is the environment that provides the stimulus and opportunity. It cannot be allowed to go stale and cease to excite, as that will directly impact on the learning.

"The environment must be rich in motives which lend interest to activity and invite the child to conduct his own experiences." **Maria Montessori**

"How can we, with our adult minds, know what will be interesting? If you follow the child...you can find out something new..." **Jean Piaget**

Recognising that learning is taking place

Learning for children needs to be holistic, it shouldn't be just about what they need to know. All learning though needs to be in a meaningful context for children, so it has a root and relevancy, which will help ensure that the child is more likely to remember and understand, as it stems from a solid base in their memories.

In Chapter 1 we looked at Prof Ferre Laevers theory relating to involvement and it is those indicators of involvement that give us clues as to whether children are engaged and learning. Learning is a constant process and starts from birth. Research into brain development shows for babies the development is rapid and:

■ Babies' brains are ready to grow and develop with masses of potential connections. All the experiences they have from the earliest days, using their abilities contributes to creating actual physical connections within the brain

■ Just because babies have limited physical skills compared with older children, it doesn't mean that their brains are less active. Consider their eyes which are absorbing all the time, it is estimated that they make three million eye movements by the time they are four months old

■ Babies and toddlers are keen to extend whatever skills they have as far as they can, they need they have to repeat actions

■ Positive emotions trigger chemicals in the brain that help to make vital connections.

Children have a thirst and desire for learning and we have to make sure that we help feed this so that it continues on a forward trajectory. We have to know when we have succeeded and equally when learning has either stagnated or is not happening.

This awareness then helps us to ensure we are providing meaningful learning experiences for the children.

Signs we know children are learning

Signs that children are learning can be in the form of a snapshot moment, or when they demonstrate memory recall from a past experience. A snapshot moment might simply be a passing comment:

A reception child in the role play area puts on a cape and says to an adult: *"I am the sun king"*, the adult replies *"I am the ice queen"*, the child responds *"I am greater, as I can melt you."*

That snapshot moment, indicates secure understanding and knowledge based on fact, which can then be used in an imaginary situation. Imagination can in many ways be an indicator not just of learning but of complex thinking, so the two combined are revealing. Role play and home corner are great places to see this happening. Here are two more examples:

A reception child in the role play area says: *"I know that superheroes can fly. Now I can learn as I have a cape on."*

A pre school child in the home corner is using the toy iron and ironing board, she goes to get some water and attempts to put some in the iron prior to using it. The child is demonstrating knowledge learnt from observing ironing at home with a steam iron.

We may also know children that children are learning from these indicators:

- Observing them building on prior experience e.g. a baby presented with different messy play experiences will always use their hands in mixed movement to explore as they understand that is how to access the experience. As they progress, the use of heir hands will also develop, by bringing them together, lifting them up, clapping hands

- Children might tell us in discussions we have with them or once they have completed a task

- A child who helps a less experienced peer

- Through our observations and assessments (further discussed in Chapter 5)

- Children who are engaged and focused on an activity for a period of time are not distracted and have a clear purpose in mind and persevere

- Children who are eager and enthusiastic and make suggestions and develop ideas

- The child's parents may tell us that their child is learning

- Obvious development in independence skills

- The child who can follow an instruction, e.g. hold the beaker with both hands

- Use of language and new vocabulary in an appropriate context.

Conversely, how can we tell if children are definitely 'not' learning? Apart from tracking through observation and assessment, there are two key indicators that learning is not happening for a child. Firstly, the aimless wanderer. If you stand back and observe your room as a whole, are there children on the edge who are just standing around? This is not the child who is new who might behave in this way, but the child who is finding nothing to interest or engage them and is not interested or stimulated by anything on offer. For these children their needs have not been met and essentially they have been overlooked. This happens quite often with children who have been in a room a while and basically they have seen and done everything. In these cases practitioners need to reflect carefully and consider where the child is developmentally and what is of interest to them and plan and provide accordingly, how can they be challenged and stimulated further?

The second key indicator is behaviour. When some children are bored they don't display it silently and passively, but they demonstrate their frustration through behaviour, seeking an alternative stimulus. As with any incident of behaviour, you should look at the reason why the behaviour is happening. Children who are stimulated and motivated to learn will be engaged and involved and therefore there are less likely to be incidents of behaviour that indicates a child is unstimulated and lacking in challenge.

This is brought about either by opportunities that do not stretch and stimulate and are by definition 'too easy', or that are too challenging. The skilfull practitioner who meets children's needs will ensure this does not happen or will know quickly how to put right.

Ofsted statement (good criteria)

Practitioners complete regular and precise assessments of children's learning that they use to effectively plan suitably challenging activities. They observe carefully, question skilfully and listen perceptively to children during activities in order to re-shape activities and give children explanations that improve their learning.

What it means / what Ofsted will be looking for

This is about how you identify and support children's learning. Activities and experiences that are planned to reflect interest and needs of the children and their responses during these planned experiences. To take opportunities to extend learning or to adapt to differing learning styles, so all children move forward.

The practitioner's influence

We consciously and inadvertently have a great influence on children's learning. Initially this is through the provision of the learning environment, to how we engage with children and the activities we provide that are adult led.

How we set up adult led activities for children, our approach and attitude has a great influence on the whether learning takes place and if that learning is meaningful and likely to be secure by knowing the children we can ensure these activities are targeted appropriately, differentiated and enable learning for the individual child.

Skilful practitioners will plan activities which motivate children by:

- Presenting tasks in imaginative ways

- Ensuring tasks are as open-ended as possible, allowing children to make choices and express their own ideas

- Using materials or story lines that children associate with play

- Providing for children's hands on, active participation.

- making available a variety of resources to enable responsive extension of learning

- reflecting and observing as the children engage, to enable consideration of how to effectively respond to the child and if that is needed.

Case study Learning in action: child and practioner working together

A child in a nursery was celebrating her birthday and brought in cakes to share with the children. She explained to the practitioner that there were 4 cakes in this pack and 4 cakes in this pack which makes 8 cakes. She didn't have the cakes in front of her, but used her hands to represent each box. She then commented further that they had bought 8 boxes.

A few minutes later the child went up to the same practitioner outside and said 'look' pointing to her coat, 'I have 4 buttons here and 4 buttons here and that makes 8 like the cakes. I do lots of counting at home.' The practitioner replied 'we can do counting here', the child asked 'do you have buttons to count', the practitioner responded 'no, but we can count the bears'.

The practitioner gets the bears, bowls and tweezers and brings to a table outside. Three children are at the table, moving the bears from a basket to the bowls, colour matching. The child goes inside to get pattern cards to match for use with the bears. She returns and hands out the cards:

P 'can I start or are we taking turns?'
C1' no, you can start'
P 'I am going to put my big bear on here'
Child one moves over and shows the practitioner what to do, putting the bears in size order,
C1 to P ' now turn it over and do this one' indicating the pattern card. The child then moves away to create her pattern.
C1 ' is that the right size?' the child questions the practitioner as she places the bear on the card
P 'what do you think?'
C1 'like this' indicating exactly how the bears needs to match and be placed on the cards
P 'yes'

The child then goes to create her own pattern
P 'the pattern goes red, red, green, green, red, red'
P to C2 'what is yours?'
C2 'red, blue, red, blue, red, blue, '
P 'that is your pattern'
C1 'my pattern is blue, blue, yellow, yellow, blue, blue'.

How did learning take place?

It is clear from the observation that the child was confident with numbers and able to do some addition and clearly has an interest in maths. The practitioner supported her learning by responding to her request about counting. However, once accessing the activity, the child decided to take it off in a different direction, she knew where to go to get the pattern cards inside and was then able to develop the learning following her own interest/idea. Having brought the cards outside she took on the role of telling and showing the practitioner what to do in the activity, demonstrating confidence and clear understanding of the purpose and process.

Although the child had initially expressed an interest in counting, it evolved through her choice into something else. The practitioner could have followed through and insisted on counting, but chose a more fluid and open approach, which enabled the child to take the lead in her own learning. The practitioner provided the initial resources and then sat back to see what the children did with the bears, rather than immediately setting up a counting experience. Children's ideas can flow and change quickly, so by being aware of that aspect of the learning process and knowing their key children, practitioners can allow them to make links and connections with previous experiences and consolidate learning.

Case study Effective, supported differentiated learning

In a 2-3 year olds room of a day nursery, a table top is covered with paper. Glue is put out for the children to use with paint brushes and glue spreaders, along with 3 small trays of coloured sand and some strips of paper and collage materials.

A child who has just turned 2 years old comes over to the table, she begins exploring the glue using a spreader on the paper covered table top. She then picks up a paintbrush and puts it into the glue and then uses it in the tray of yellow sand. She moves it backwards and forwards repeatedly, then stabs into the glue.

Another child who has just turned 2 years old joins the table, standing next to the practitioner. He takes a glue spreader with glue and moves it around on the paper. The practitioner pinches some green coloured sand and demonstrates how to lift and sprinkle, he tries this a couple of times, sprinkling on his glue. He sees that the practitioner is demonstrating using the paintbrush with glue in the sand tray, as she copies what the first child is doing, he tries this, but then returns to his exploration of the glue with the glue spreader. He continues just freely exploring in his world for some time, repeated actions feeding his fascination.

Two older children join in, who are nearly three, she wants her own paper to stick on. The practitioner goes to get some and some additional junk resources, therefore enabling differentiated learning. The practitioner also gets scissors and offers a pair to the child exploring the glue next to her. The older children take strips of paper with faces printed on them, the practitioner explains about cutting down so they could stick the faces.

The two year old tries to cut looking at what the older children are doing, he tries and tries, persisting without succeeding, but he is not deterred. He looks to the practitioner who gives him a thinner, smaller strip, he persists keeping on trying putting the scissors repeatedly to the card. The practitioner holds up some florist ribbon, he gestures to it, the practitioner says 'you want to cut this?' she holds out the ribbon to the child and he then attempts to cut. He takes the ribbon from her and keeps on trying to cut.

What the practitioner did

The practitioner was relatively silent, just giving gentle encouragement to the younger children, every so often using colour vocabulary and parallel talk 'are you trying to stick it down?'

What the practitioner said

The activity had been set up as some children were reluctant to get anything on their hands and she wanted to enable them to use tools to explore. The first two children to experience the activity were new to the room, so free exploration was essential. They had previously tried crazy foam and rolling pins but the children weren't keen.

Why and how did learning take place

Learning was effective for all the children as they were able to access the activity at their level and this was enabled and supported by the adult. She did not intervene at any point, but let the children direct their own learning and was there if needed. Her lack of direct intervention and lack of talk, enabled the youngest child to become fully absorbed and concentrate for a long period of time on a task at which he was not successful in terms of outcome, but in the process was discovering about persistence and resilience. Had the practitioner intervened, his concentration would have been interrupted and perhaps he would have been supported to do something that developmentally he was ready to do.

When the older children joined the activity she added additional resources to meeting their needs, enable different learning opportunities for them.
With this activity the covering of the table with paper enabled the younger children to explore in an unrestricted way, they needed the space for large movements. It was interesting that the older child requested her own paper, as she clearly had a plan for her own piece of work and developmentally did not need the space, her fine and gross motor skills would enable her to create on a smaller scale.

Case study Learning taking place

The activity

In a pre school some children were working collaboratively on the floor to make a large elephant from boxes. Two children were creating the face, they decided they needed to make eyes. The practitioner told them to think about what they needed, what they eyes might look like and to get the necessary resources. The children collected white paper, pencils, scissors and glue. The drew two eye shapes on paper, cut them out and stuck them onto the elephant's face. This was entirely their own work. Another child was painting the mouth, the practitioner discussed with him the colour, he decided on pink. They then had a discussion about whether he wanted to use the ready mixed pink paint or make his own. He opted to make his own pink, taking a paint palette and the white and pink paint, he created his own colour and commented on how he felt he hadn't quite got the shade right, and needed more white.

What learning took place

Firstly, all three children were enabled and encouraged to be independent learners making choices and decisions for themselves. They were able to work out a plan from an idea, consider what was needed and follow it through to its conclusion. All three children were building on previous experience to access the activity. They demonstrated the characteristics of effective learning in action.

Case study Learning taking place

In a baby room in a day nursery, a splash mat is out on the floor and damp sand and powder paint are placed on the mat. The babies are stripped to their nappies and encouraged to explore. The practitioner models, saying 'mix together', 'where has it all gone?' and then sits back, offering an emotional support from her presence if needed. A child is looking, but is reluctant to join in, so the practitioner puts some of the sand mix on the child's hand to feel and the child squeezes it. The child watches and then walks onto the mat, she moves her feet in the sand mix, then picks some up in her hand and then sits down and giggles. The children are all engaged covering themselves with the sand mix, using their hands and feet. The practitioner lifts up some sand and sprinkles.

What the practitioner said

The activity was provided as they were introducing new experiences and situations to the children and it was a follow on from similar previous experiences with other media and materials. To extend the practitioner felt she could add water, but that wouldn't have been necessary as the children were fully engaged.

What learning took place and why

The practitioners did not interfere or bombard the children with questions or language, they just let them explore freely. The children were using their whole bodies to explore, and sensory development was stimulated. They were independent as they controlled their own experience and were given freedom. This in turn would support confidence and self esteem, particularly in relation to trying out new experiences.

Case study Maths activity - missed learning opportunities

In a pre school room of a day nursery, 5 children are sitting with a practitioner. They are looking at numbers on wooden tiles.

P 'we can use numbers to tell the time, what time do you go to bed?'
The children respond with various times 9pm, 6pm, 2pm, 10pm not all children respond.
P 'You said 9pm Rory, can you find me the number 9' he finds the tile
P 'can you count out 9 counters Rory?'

Eventually all the children have a wooden tile (not necessarily linked to the time they said they went to bed). They begin to count out the number of counters to match their number tile.

Rory counts out his tiles '8', the practitioner asks 'is that enough?', he replies 'no', he gets another counter.

The practitioner then returns to the idea of numbers being all around and using them to tell the time and gets the clock down from the wall. She ten suggests each child writes their number after counting out the counters. To one child she says ' you have found your number, counted counters, written your number, what could you do now?' the child thinks, but does not respond, the practitioner suggests writing a number line from 1-10.

Gradually interest wanes and the children move away from the table.

What the practitioner said

The practitioner said the activity had been planned as a next step, as they had enjoyed an activity the previous week writing numbers on a white board with pens and they enjoyed talking about numbers generally and had made a height chart.

What learning took place

The children had an opportunity to recognise a number and then the quantitive value of that number was reinforced as they counted out the correct number of counters. The first child Rory knew he needed one more than eight to make nine.

How the activity could be developed and improved

Initially, some learning took place for the children, but there was no clear focus to the activity and it was not differentiated. The practitioner, by asking the children what time they went to bed and using that number, had no control as to whether the number was appropriate for them, in terms of their understanding of the quantitive value of number. Also the numbers were out of context, which was suitable for some of the children but not all of them. The children enjoyed counting out the correct number of counters to match the number, so this element of the activity could have been the main focus, helping to reinforce the quantitive value of numbers and their order. That could then have been differentiated for those children able to consider 'one more than' and for the initial counting, taken into account their knowledge of number.

Case study Learning not taking place

In a pre school with 2-4 year olds, the theme is the rain forest, an activity is set up to make venus fly traps. The children are given pre cut out and folded paper plates. They are told to paint the inside of the plate red and the outside green. This is a one to one activity. A child sits and waits painting around the rim of a paint pot.

Why is learning not taking place?

The theme has no context or relevance for the children, as they have no concept of what a venus fly trap is. To them it is just a dull painting activity. They are not required to

use their imaginations or develop any creativity. It is simply a going through the motions painting activity where they are told what to do. There is no opportunity for the activity to develop and is simply a conveyer belt.

Could the activity be improved?

Apart from simply setting up a free painting activity. If the practitioner wanted to look at venus fly traps with the children, this would have been better done through pictures and books.

Case study **Learning not taking place**

In a baby room the children are painting using brushes on pieces of white A4 paper, they have been given yellow paint only to paint flowers.

Why is learning not taking place?

Babies need to explore paint first with their hands and bodies. Large tools and paintbrushes shouldn't be used until much later on. It is about understanding the properties of paint and exploring it from a sensory perspective. They need a large area to explore the paint as their arms and hands move around. Developmentally, they are not at a stage to be able to relate their movements to paint with a specific object.

How could the activity be improved?

Just enabling the babies to explore paint on a table top or on the floor in a large space using their whole bodies or hands, with no emphasis on an end product just the process of enjoying exploring the paint.

As well as how we set up activities, we also need to consider how we manage group times, are they supportive of learning? Are the children physically comfortable? What is the focus is it appropriate for all the children?

Learning cannot take place if children are physically uncomfortable. If they are sitting on the floor do they have sufficient space? Can they stretch out their legs or lie down? Do they have special designated place to sit e.g. on a cushion or a carpet square? Are they sitting in a circle or semi circle so they feel engaged and involved? Do you split large groups of children to ensure you can pitch your story or chat to the level of the children in the group? This is particularly important in pre schools who may have 2 to 4 year olds together in the same room.

Supporting children's learning

Reflecting in detail on an activity you have carried out with the children is important for reflecting on your own practice and to enable further learning opportunities for the children. These questions guide you through an activity analysis.

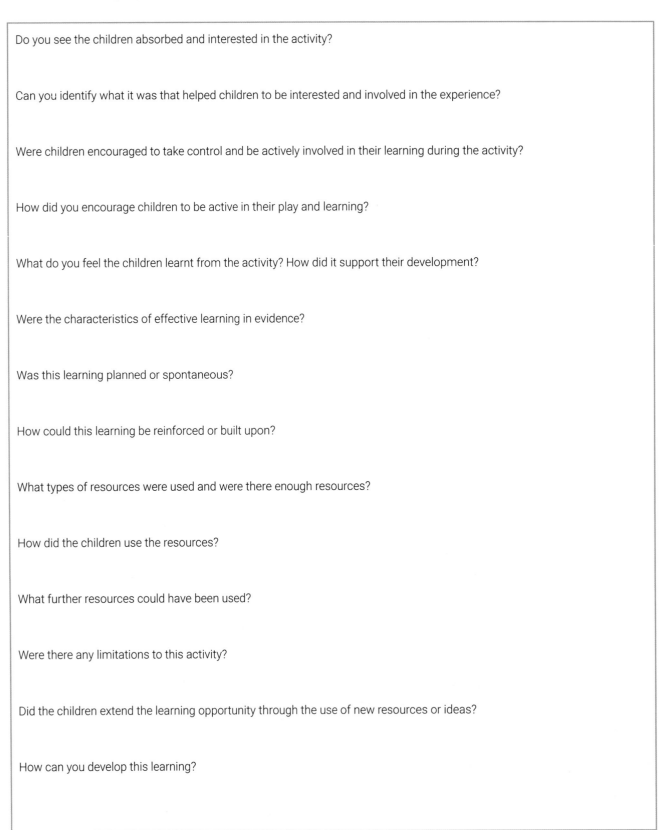

Do you see the children absorbed and interested in the activity?

Can you identify what it was that helped children to be interested and involved in the experience?

Were children encouraged to take control and be actively involved in their learning during the activity?

How did you encourage children to be active in their play and learning?

What do you feel the children learnt from the activity? How did it support their development?

Were the characteristics of effective learning in evidence?

Was this learning planned or spontaneous?

How could this learning be reinforced or built upon?

What types of resources were used and were there enough resources?

How did the children use the resources?

What further resources could have been used?

Were there any limitations to this activity?

Did the children extend the learning opportunity through the use of new resources or ideas?

How can you develop this learning?

This sequence of three photos clearly illustrate how an adult is supporting a child, scaffolding their learning and then moving away.

In the first photo the adult is supporting the child to weave the ribbon through the railings, demonstrating the technique. She is guiding the child to develop and support her skill development.

In the second photo, the child's confidence is built and had understanding of technique in place. The adult has moved away and the child competently works alone.

The final photo shows the child's final design achieved by the weaving activity.

It is not necessary for the adult to remain with the child once the technique and process have been understood. By working independently the child will gain a greater understanding, with time to reflect and critically analyse their actions.

Planning effective adult led activities

Firstly you need to ask yourself, 'Is this an opportunity for children to find their own ways to represent and develop their own ideas?' (Development Matters, page 7)

Then remember the following:

- The emphasis should be on the process and not the end product

- Plan carefully and think about differentiation for individuals

- Allow the children to explore within the activity

- See yourself as a facilitator and supporter

- Show interest and enjoyment yourself

- Follow the child's lead

- Respond to 'in the moment' teaching opportunities

- Don't control or direct

- Give children time to think and reflect

- Evaluate and reflect yourself, considering what the children did and learnt and if any follow up is needed.

Meeting individual children's needs to support learning

The concept of 'meeting needs' is mentioned and referred to very frequently as a way to ensure we are supporting children's learning, but what exactly does it mean? Whilst all children follow the same pattern and order of development, they develop at different rates, therefore all have individual development and learning needs. A child's key carer needs to be aware of where a child currently is at, where they need to move to next with their development, combined with what is of particular interest to them. This combination is about their individual learning needs. A skilled practitioner will plan to meet these needs through providing different experiences for the child, tracking and evaluating their progress, identifying any gaps and considering how best to support them to move forward.

Key principles of learning

To learn effectively, children need:

To feel valued, cared for, safe, secure in moving between home and the school/setting, confident;

To develop independence, self esteem, positive attitudes to learning, skills and competencies, individual talents, positive relationships;

To experience interactions with peers and adults, a balance of experiences, new opportunities in a stimulating environment, a wide range of practical activities, opportunities for exploration and investigation, success which is recognised and acknowledged. It is our responsibility, as part of meeting children's individual needs, that we enable all the above and provide accordingly.

Children need to develop a range of skills in order to learn and these are generally facilitated through the experiences that we provide.

The list below identifies the various ways in which children learn. It is a broad list and children will use different combinations at any one time.
The list can be used as an effective starting point for reviewing the variety of opportunities for learning on offer to the children. Where can each be experienced in the environment? Indoors and outdoors? Are there any which are not effectively provided? What improvements and developments are required?

- Listening
- Questioning
- Selecting
- Reasoning
- Participating
- Reflecting
- Recording
- Comparing/contrasting
- Recalling
- Describing
- Discussing
- Researching
- Analysing
- Perceiving
- Predicting
- Observing
- Planning
- Problem solving
- Organising
- Communicating

- Expressing
- Negotiating
- Concentrating
- Exploring
- Adapting
- Initiating
- Decision making
- Experimenting
- Creating
- Designing
- Estimating
- Interacting
- Pattern making
- Perseverance
- Imagining
- Manipulating
- Cooperating
- Sorting
- Sequencing

We should remember that children learn when:

- They feel happy secure and relaxed
- They are successful
- Their efforts are acknowledged and praised
- They are encouraged to try
- Adults are well motivated and supported
- Activities are appropriate, relevant and related to interest
- They know what is expected of them
- You are interested in them
- They are ready
- They are not too tired
- Adults know them well and facilitate meaningful learning opportunities
- Activities reflect their interests, needs and development.

How young children learn

This table identifies some of the key ways in which children learn and how we enable learning to take place.

Young children learn if...	How we enable...
■ Concentration spans are expanded	■ Through a routine that allows children time to wallow in experiences and by providing experiences that tap into their interests and natural curiosity.
■ They are interested in what they do	■ Children are often interested simply in every day experiences.
■ Expectations are high	■ Adults need to have high expectations, that encourage children to achieve beyond their current level of development, to ensure they don't stagnate.
■ The environment is stimulating and appropriate	■ This is the immediate stimulus (see Chapter 3)
■ They feel valued	■ We show children that they are valued through giving them our time, getting to know them, by displaying their work, by ensuring they have a sense of belonging in the setting.
■ The practitioner shows that their opinion matters	■ This links with British Values and is about, for example, enabling children to make choices about what they would like to do, and us reflecting these opinions in the provision and in planning accordingly.
■ Activities are matched to their individual stage of development	■ Ensuring the planning cycle is in place and that individual needs are met.
■ They are engaged in something is fun	■ If it is fun and enjoyable learning is much more likely to happen.
■ Everyone involved understands how learning takes place	■ Adults understand how children learn and children are supported to recognise their achievements.

Schemas

Children also learn through schemas and these, when recognised, can also be a clear indicator that learning is taking place. A schema is a repeated pattern of behaviour that can be observed in children's play.

Schemas are an intrinsic part of child development. They are important to our understanding of how some children learn. Knowing about schemas offers a positive view of children's actions and enables parents and practitioners to make sense of what children are doing.

Knowledge of schemas and understanding schematic behaviour in young children can help practitioners to:

■ Understand why children are doing certain things, gain a clearer insight of their interests

■ Describe children's actions and behaviours in new ways which can be enabled through a reflective and clearer understanding of their motivations

■ Support parents' understanding of their children's learning

■ Inform planning for children's individual interests, preoccupations and abilities using their schema to promote learning

■ Be more effective in supporting children's learning through extension of thought and modelling of language, and the provision of enjoyable experiences that stimulate and interest them

■ Provide real and first-hand experiences for exploration and experimentation

■ Enable repetition of opportunities that will be interesting and relevant to the child

■ Consider if a schema is having influence on any inappropriate behaviour, so outlets can be provided to channel this behaviour appropriately.

Once a schema has been recognised in a child, it is a fascinating process to observe them and see how it is reflected in their actions and providing further opportunities through resourcing for them to explore their schema. From this we can learn more about how the child uses the pattern of behaviour within the schema as a learning tool.

Schemas explained

Schema	What it means	Possible behaviours	How the practitioner can support
Transporting	Moving resources and self from place to place.	A child may carry all the bricks from one place to another in a bag, the sand from the tray to the home corner in a bucket, push a friend around in a toy pram.	Provide shopping bags, wheelbarrows, trollies, buggies, trailers, trucks, baskets, wheeled boxes.
Enveloping	Covering themselves or other items.	A child may cover themselves in a flannel when washing, wrap dolls and toys up in blankets and fabric, cover their painting with one colour.	Provide resources for wrapping presents, practising wrapping things around with ribbons or tape or putting letters into envelopes, have dressing up clothes, hats and scarves available for putting layers on, den making and boxes.
Rotation	Exploring things that turn, including self.	Interested in wheels and cogs; likes twirling and twisting themselves, enjoys spinning round or being swung around; runs in circles; rolls down a hill, turns taps on and off, draws circles, likes to watch fans, washing machines and whisks in movement, reaches for round objects near them, he likes to watch ball rolling.	Provide hoops and tyres to roll around, play parachute and circle games; provide toys which have moving parts to turn around, provide spinning tops, clocks, kaleidoscope and water wheels; roll with rolling pins; make windmills; use stickers for decoration; talk about shapes.
Trajectory	Learning about movement of things and self in vertical, horizontal and diagonal lines, still and in motion.	Drops things form high chair or cot; throws things; may gaze at your face; lines things up; climbs up and over; jumps off furniture; runs up and down; draws or paints lines; follows lines painted on the floor/ground; plays with running water in the bathroom; likes to go through tunnels; makes trails with glue; pushes cars or pushchairs in a straight line; knocks over structures built by other children.	Provide balls of different sizes; build slopes and ramps to roll things down; provide target throwing opportunities; provide a variety of building bricks and other resources to build towers and knock them down; play with running water, woodwork, have available percussion instruments; provide opportunities to experience space and movement in/out, to move under, climb up, move across; play with ribbons waving them up/down or side to side; begin to introduce language of 'over/under', fast/slow, high/low; provide leaves or feathers to watch them falling down, etc.
Enclosing/ containing	Surrounding self, objects or space with a border.	Plays with farm animals and makes fences for them; builds enclosures with bricks and puts objects inside; puts cars in a garage, may draw a line around their picture; likes to sit inside a space such as basket, box or tyre; may surround themselves with cushions, may fill up containers.	Provide peg boards to make borders or Duplo boards for building houses: provide resources to make borders on paper and 3-D; barrels and tunnels are good for hiding in as are den building materials and pieces of fabric. Ensure access to small world play with fences, wooden blocks for making enclosures.
Connecting	Joining and separating items and objects, both those designed to be connected and those the child tries to connect.	Gives and collects objects from adult; enjoys construction toys which involve joining things together e.g. magnetic blocks, stickle bricks; takes things apart, joins the table and chair by sticking tape across; ties a string to crates or bikes.	Provide construction toys which connect, train set with linked carriages, tape of different sorts, pegs and string to connect items together, provide ribbon to weave in and out of resources, plumbing pipes and connectors, locks and chains to practise connecting.
Positioning	Placing objects or themselves in particular places, carefully and precisely.	Lies on the floor or under a table; may put things on their head; walks around the edge of a sandpit; prefers to have food items separated on a plate; enjoys lining up cars and threading beads/buttons; likes to stand at the front or back of a line.	Provide tyres, crates and boxes in different places and at different heights for children to position themselves or objects in; provide tins or wooden boxes and pegs for positioning around.
Transforming	Enjoys the process of changing the appearance or state of something.	Likes to see, manipulates and explores changes with dry/wet materials; may add juice to their mashed potato; likes to mix sand and water.	Provide a variety of malleable materials; let children mix paints, add colour to cornflour or water to clay; engage children in cooking activities; explain changes, etc.

Observation are key to recognising if children are and possibly what they are learning. Of course, we can't always know exactly what they are learning as it will be in their minds and may only become evident at a later time. By standing back and observing what is happening we learn a great deal about it, much more than if we attempt to be involved. It is about sitting back and letting the story of the learning evolve. This doesn't necessarily mean recorded observations, in fact the majority of the time it won't be, it will simply be what you see and hear. Key to this is an open mind, we need to be prepared to be surprised and to see and witness or hear the unexpected, not predict.

Learning for children can be incidental, obscure and random, it will not be ordered, neat and organised. This is also why, when we plan an adult led activity, we may have an idea of how it links to the EYFS and what the outcomes might be, but this does not mean that is what the child will take away.

Learning for children, especially the youngest is very much in the moment, therefore the skilful practitioner will respond there and then to facilitate further learning based on what they have observed. There is no point waiting as the moment will have passed.

Babies and young children are experiencing and learning in the here and now, not storing up their questions until tomorrow or next week. It is in that moment of curiosity, puzzlement, effort or interest – the 'teachable moment' – that the skilful adult makes a difference.
Playing, Learning and Interacting DCSF 2009

Following the children's lead to support learning

Following the children's lead is one of the most effective ways of supporting learning. By doing that we are ensuring that learning is meaningful to them.

Following the child's lead

In a pre school a child is playing with some coloured cubes, organising them into columns. He comments "I wonder what would happen if we mixed this colour with this colour" indicating green and red. The practitioner suggests that they go over to the craft area and get some red and green paint and mix them to see what happens.

The above observation clearly illustrates how a practitioner took the opportunity to follow a child's lead and extend their learning. The child expressed a thought, an interest and she went with his idea.
The immediacy of the response meant that the learning potential was optimised and the child gained.

Extension of learning is a critical part of teaching in the early years. Children are learning at a rapid rate and are inquisitive and curious, our challenge is to respond. Extension of learning might be about going off following a child's idea or observations in an adult led activity, adding extra resources to the continuous provision, setting a challenge or responding to an interest.

It can also be about observing what children are doing in their self initiated play and how this can be extended further with focused learning in an adult led activity. This is particularly relevant for older children and it should be explained to them by the practitioner that they saw them, for example, making pizza with the play dough, so you have set up an activity to make real pizza. An activity building on a child initiated experience, would need to be implemented either that day or the next day (depending on the activity), so the relevancy and follow on is there for the children.

Differentiation is also a key element of extension of learning and as children get older, particularly in reception, and are having more focused maths and literacy, input is essential.

Differentiation is about presenting a task in different ways to groups of children to meet their particular learning needs and ensuring it is at their level, but with the potential to extend. Often with younger children an activity will naturally differentiate itself as the children access it at the level they are at, as their development stage allows, if it is presented in an open style. This then means that the emphasis is on the process and discovery and it is not controlled or too focused on a specific outcome or purpose.

If we do not endeavour to extend learning for children, experiences become static and dull and learning potential is not fulfilled.

> *'Development can only take place when children are actively involved, when they are occupied with a high, non stop degree of concentration, when they are interested, when they give themselves completely, when they use all their (mental) abilities, to invent and make new things and when this gives them a high degree of satisfaction and pleasure.'* Ferre Laevers

Challenge

To move forward and to further develop, children need to be challenged physically, emotionally and intellectually. Day to day life can pose those challenges, but our role is to enhance those to specifically meet the needs of children through planned activities and in challenge posed through resources, therefore extending learning and promoting critical thinking and problem solving.

How we might challenge:

- Through provocations (see Chapter 3)

- Creating a problem to be solved

- Through suggestion

- Asking an open-ended question

- Making a change within the learning environment

- Doing something different with the resources.

Without challenge, learning cannot move forwards and will become stagnant. Children can seek challenge for themselves through opportunity and access to the environment, as ideas and connections evolve in their minds, but to keep this moving and fresh, we need to continually reflect on the opportunities for challenge.

In the indicators for involvement, Laevers uses the phrase 'edge of capabilities', this is exactly where we want our

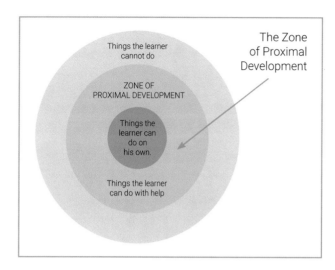

children to be: at the edge of their capabilities. Being on the edge is exciting: can you go further? Can you do more? Children will be eager, wanting to reach higher. That can be hard to quantify, however through careful observation and assessment, we should be able to ascertain if each child is enabled to challenge themselves as far as possible. Do we as practitioners have high expectations for each child? Do we enable them to find their own potential and move beyond it? Laevers 'edge of capability' links with Vygotsky's theory of the zone of proximal development. Vygotsky stated that each child has the potential to move forward to a new starting point within their zone of potential with support from an adult or more experienced peer. Children need to be supported to move into the zone of proximal development, so they do not stagnate and learning continues. As well as supporting children ourselves by extending their learning, we also need to support them to become independent learners. It is about a balance between supported learning and independence, which is illustrated in the example of the child accessing the junk modelling.

Case study Modelling

A junk modelling activity is set up and a child comes over to join in. The practitioner says to her, 'think about what you want to make and choose your boxes'. The child stops and thinks, selects her resources and begins to create. Later, as the child is fixing two awkwardly shaped items together, the practitioner says to her 'think about what will work best to fix them, glue or tape?' Here, the child is encouraged to be reactive about her choices and to make informed decisions. The practitioner, through questions and suggestions, enabled the child to make a plan and to consider how best to execute it. The practitioner supported the child to move into a zone of proximal development, extending the learning. As a consequence, the child remained at this activity for around an hour as she worked carefully to build her model.

Case study Vygotsky in action

In the outside area of a day nursery children from both the toddler room and pre school are playing. A group of pre school children are filling up a bucket of water, using various containers. As the bucket is filled the practitioner lifts it up and pours the water onto their drain pipe water wall. The children are delighted and ask her to lift the bucket higher. This carries on for quite a while and some of the younger children stand and watch. Eventually everyone leaves apart from one child. He picks up a small plastic tea cup, fills it with water, reaches up as high as he can and pours the water onto the water wall. He stands back and says with excitement 'look at the water coming down'. He repeats this action many times, on each occasion standing back and repeating the words. He is fascinated that his actions have made the water 'come down'.

Why is this Vygotsky in action?

The child with the tea cup had observed the older children's play and wanted to try it himself. Through his observation he understood the basic principle of what he needed to do, unable to handle the bucket he uses a tea cup. Vygotsky's theory of the zone of proximal development, considers that children can achieve more through support from older peers or adults. In this instance the child observed the adult and older children and worked out how to access the experience for himself and make the water 'come down'. Had he not observed their actions, he might not have had the idea or been able to work out how to use the water wall. The repeated action meant he was able to test out his theory and plan numerous times and therefore consolidate the concept and learning in his mind.

'In play a child always behaves beyond his average age, above his daily behaviour; in play it is as though he were a head taller than himself.' **Lev Vygotsky**

The above quote from Vygotsky explaining the significance for children of play and in essence learning, is clearly illustrated in the above observation.

Involving parents in children's learning

We need to look at ways in which we can involve parents in children's learning at home, so we can work together; this can then act as a further tool for extending and broadening learning. If what is learnt in the setting is reinforced or developed at home, then that learning is more likely to become consolidated in the child's mind and can be expanded upon. For this to be effective and to benefit the child, there are key strategies to consider.

Involving parents with play

- Take time to get to know parents so you can share information and ideas that are appropriate to their level of confidence, as well as relevant to their interests, culture and family life

- Treat parents as partners in their children's learning – parents are more likely to listen to information and advice if they feel respected and valued

- Model positive interaction with children – for instance talk to the child about what they have been doing during the day and praise them in front of their parent when they arrive

to collect their child. Chatting to children, praising them and showing an interest in their play are all vital ways with which parents can support their learning and development

- Talk to parents about what their child has enjoyed doing during the day and share information about what they have been learning through this kind of play activity

- Talk to parents about what their child enjoys doing at home. Let them know how important they are for their child's learning and explore how they could join in play activities at home together

- Help parents to see that the aim of playing with their child is to have fun together and build their child's confidence by allowing them to take the lead. Many parents use play as an opportunity to 'teach' their children a new skill and may need to be reassured that children learn best at their own pace

- Involve parents in activities to support home learning where appropriate

- Let parents know if their child talks about a play activity that they did at home and how much they seemed to get out of this time with their parent.

Practical ideas for involving parents in children's learning at home

- Put suggestions on display boards of children's work

- Include suggestions in newsletters, for activities parents can do at home with their children.

- Have a resource bank of activity cards with suggestions e.g. how many round things can you find in your home? Can you draw around the feet of all the people who live with you? What number is on your front door? A play dough recipe, how to make a jigsaw from a cereal box, count how many socks long you are, etc...

- Information leaflets about how parents can support children's independence and self help skills at home

- Have a resource library of simple activities parents can take home to do with their children e.g. simple games, mark making materials, collage

- Encourage parents to share what they have done with their children at home, with photos or displays.

Assessment

For learning to be effective, appropriate and real, we need to reflect and assess prior learning that has taken place. We assess children's learning all the time, both formally and informally, to identify if it is taking place, what learning is happening and how we can move them on. The more formal assessment we carry out gives us a clear picture of exactly where a child is and where we would like them to go next. There are two forms of assessment, **formative** which is your observations and **summative** assessment which is the conclusion you make about a child's progress based on your knowledge of the child and what you have learnt about the child's development and learning through observations. So for assessment to be effective you need quality observations.

Quality observations:

- Are embedded in every day practice to build up an accurate picture of the unique child

- May include spontaneous, narrative and digitally recorded observations

- Are purposeful, informative and positive to capture how children learn, what children know, can do, are currently interested in and demonstrates their current stage of development

- Are completed in a range of contexts, for example in their independent play, during everyday routines and when engaged with others

- Reflect multiple perspectives - the child, their family and practitioners

- Begins with key settling observations.

'Observation entails close attention to children's behaviour within particular contexts, followed by assessment involving reflection and evaluation in terms of children's knowledge, skills, well-being and thinking. Planning is the response that is intended to support, challenge or extend the learning.' Nancy Stewart, 2011

What is evident is that when observations are combined with practitioner knowledge of the child, a much more realistic and informed assessment judgement can be made. The first full assessment is the starting point, and is completed after a child has been in a setting for about 3 or 4 weeks, and is settled. This starting points assessment is key to the whole process of assessment, as it forms the basis from which progress is monitored during the child's time in the setting, answering the key question, has progress been made?

Assessment needs to be reflective and should not be reliant on highlighted checklists which give only part of the story and essentially require children to fit into boxes, which is not going to happen. The checklists may be used as a guide, but there will always be things you see a child do, interesting and insightful, that are not listed on any checklist. Equally, there may be something stated on the checklist that you never see a child do, common sense and practitioner knowledge should prevail.

Ofsted statement (good criteria)	What it means / what Ofsted will be looking for
Practitioners have high expectations of all children based on accurate assessment of children's skills, knowledge and understanding when they join the setting.	A clear and precise starting points assessment for all children, practitioners who challenge children and stimulate their curiosity and learning ensuring they make progress. This will be preceded by an initial assessment completed with parents on entry.
The key person system works effectively to engage parents, including those who may be more reluctant to contribute in their children's learning. Parents contribute to initial assessments of children's starting points on entry and they are kept informed about their children's progress. Parents are encouraged to support and share information about their children's learning and development at home.	Parents contributions to an initial assessment, so you can see if there is anything the child can do at home that you have not seen in the setting. This exchange of information needs to be ongoing and evidenced with invited comments on summative assessments, and/or observations from home. There should also be in evidence effective strategies, how you support and encourage parents to help their children at home, with evidence of where this has happened.

Quality assessment

- To incorporate the prime areas of learning and development for all children and include the specifc areas as appropriate

- Include observation of both child initiated and adult led experiences

- Emphasis on what children can do and what they can nearly do

- A range and variety of observations to work with

- Time to reflect and draw conclusions

- Evidence of the process and not just the product, it is in the 'doing' that the learning and development takes place.

From assessment we should be able to identify the following:

- The needs of the child in terms of planning the environment and specific experiences

- Identify what they can do, can nearly do and what they need to be able to do to develop further

- Provide information about their level of play, development, interest and interactions with others

- Any areas that need specific focus.

A summative assessment is exactly that, a summary, a description of what the child has achieved in the areas of learning and development, based on observation and practitioner knowledge, it should be personal and reflect the child's personality and achievements. It is also essential that you identify where the child is at in the development phases for each of the aspects of the areas. The aspects need to be identified individually as a child might not be in the same development phase for each aspect of an area.

Summative assessment enables us to forward plan, thinking over the next period of time what we hope the child will achieve in each of the seven areas. It is important that if we have any concerns about a child's progress in the prime areas, we need to identify clearly how we are going to address this issue and support the child to move forward. All summative assessments should be shared with parents, so they can work with us to support the child. This becomes even more imperative if there are concerns about progress in any of the prime areas.

Having identified what we hope the individual child will achieve over the next term or 4 month period, we need to consider how this is provided through the continuous provision. Are any enhancements or additions needed? Might there be specific planned adult led activities which could help? Are there particular resources the child might need to access? These overview next steps might relate to the development of specific skills e.g. use of scissors or doing up their coat. It might be about being able to make choices about their play, or becoming more resilient at overcoming obstacles.

It should not be just about following statements from development matters or the early years outcomes, it needs to be holistic and about what each child specifically needs. This does not mean these next steps are all you focus on, but are simply a guide to enable effective support for the child and give you an indication of what to look out for, and remember they might be achieved very quickly. We need to ensure we are responding to the children's evolving learning needs.

We can't always predict accurately where a child will go next, although based on development theory we can have a good idea. We need to continually evaluate, to respond to the evolving learning and development needs of individual children.

Observation and assessment reflective practice questions

These questions can be used to reflect on the quality of the observation and assessment systems in your setting.

Observation

What is it like for a child here?

Are all practitioners responding to observations about children's progress?

Assessment

How are children's starting points assessed?

Who is involved in this process?

Do children and parents have a voice in the assessment process? How?

Are our tracking systems effectively building a picture of a child's progress?

How do we seek and share assessment information with parents? Is it effective?

How are interventions put in place to support all children and enable them to succeed?

How do we build effective relationships with other professionals?

What difference are we making and how do we know? Are we narrowing the gap?

Northamptonshire Early Years

Cohort tracking

All summative assessments having been completed, the data then needs to be collated to assess the progress of the cohort. The purpose of this is to identify if there are any specific groups of children making more or less progress in specific areas of learning and development. You can then use the data to do comparisons between the progress of boys, girls, children with EAL, any children with additional needs and children in receipt of Early Years Pupil Premium funding.

The information from this data should then be analysed to see if any action is necessary. It might identify gaps within the provision, practitioner skills and understanding of how to support particular children or learning in particular areas or it might flag up a lack of observations reflecting a specific area of learning and development. I had an incident in a setting where we were looking at the tracker and it identified children were making less

progress in personal, social and emotional development. This did not reflect what was happening in the setting and the manager said it showed her that her staff were not recording many observations on PSED and were too reliant on information from observations and not complimented with their knowledge when completing summative assessments.

An action plan should be made based on the data from the cohort tracking, clearly identifying actions to be taken and what the expected **impact** of these actions will be; once implemented this should be followed through with a **review** which identifies what the actual impact of these actions was on both the children and the setting.

Did the actions make a difference? Did they have a positive impact on the children? This is then followed through in the next cohort analysis to see the effect on progression.

Enthusiasm for the cohort analysis

Working with day nursery managers and discussing with them their cohort analysis, this is what I have discovered about the cohort analysis:

- It is illuminating and revealing

- Makes you reflect on the quality of observations and what is recorded

- Gives pause for thought over practitioner knowledge and awareness

- Can give you surprises

- Clearly identifies areas where children are making more or less progress

- Using percentages with results helps to highlight

- Provides key information for developing practice

- It is essential for managers to review the summative assessments informing the cohort analysis

- Will back up what you discover through room and staff observations.

Cohort analysis in action (comment for practice)

The use of the cohort analysis for me as a nursery manager is becoming invaluable. A recent room observation in the 2-3s room revealed that the staff skill in using open-ended and meaningful questioning appeared to be limited. In turn, this presented less opportunities for the children to develop their speaking skills. Following on from this, the Spring Term Cohort Analysis appeared to confirm this, 33% of the children in this age range were below the expected level. This meant the staff now had a clear focus going forward to develop the curriculum to include those opportunities, but also for me as the nursery manager to recognise a potential gap in the staff abilities and therefore plan for appropriate continued professional development.
Tracey Heayns, Nursery Manager

We need to use the information from the cohort to guide us in identifying key areas in the environment, regarding practice and children's learning. This focus enables further progression for children and works towards narrowing the gap with those that are making progress and those making less progress.

When carrying out the analysis, we need to also be realistic, remembering there can be discrepancies with development and we need to think about the whole child and personal factors that can affect development, e.g. the child who is the youngest of four children in their family, perhaps their language is not as far forward as you would expect, could this be to do with the opportunity to talk at home, lots of competition. Consideration should also be given to the child's personality. It is more than just analysing data, but also considering influencing factors.

Effective extension of children's learning is a combination of several factors working together. The individual practitioner and the team using their knowledge and expertise, to provide an effective learning environment, which stimulates and interests the children and meets their needs. The practitioners using sensitive and appropriate teaching methods, to support and extend learning, either in the moment or through planned activities. Careful observation carried out by practitioners, feed into assessment, alongside their knowledge of the child, to gain a clear insight into progress and how to continue that process, ensuring learning is continually moving forward.

'The teacher's task is first to nourish and assist, to watch, encourage, guide, induce, rather than to interfere, prescribe or restrict.' **Maria Montessori**

For consideration

When looking at cohort tracking for analysis, remember to reflect on how the prime areas impact on the specific areas. An issue with a specific area might be more to do with progress in a prime area, especially if it relates to language.

For example, if you look at the aspect 'The World' in 'Understanding the World', much in the 30-50 month age phase relates to description, explaining and language. So a child whose language development is not at the expected level, whilst having the intellectual knowledge, might appear to have not achieved as much progress in that aspect. It is therefore important to look at all significant factors.

As well as reflecting on individual children, it is important to additionally use the cohort analysis as a tool to support continuous quality improvement.

This can be reflected upon considering these key areas of focus:

- the effectiveness of the manager in helping underperforming practitioners to support the children's learning and development effectively

- targeting professional development needs for individual practitioners, which might be training or on the job coaching

- identifying possible whole staff training needs, perhaps relating to knowledge gaps in identifying learning in practice

- the strength of the key person relationship and the depth of understanding about each child

- the effectiveness of the monitoring of learning journals/observations.

Children's experiences in each area of learning

Creative and imaginative experiences can be about:

- Allowing children the freedom to express ideas, feelings and understanding through art, music, movement, imaginative play, stories and poetry

- Encouraging an understanding of colours and textures through the use of paint, collage materials and mark making tools

- Experimenting and exploring possibilities with a variety of media

- Practising and developing the skills necessary for creativity

- Appreciating and valuing the creations of others

- Selecting and comparing

- Using music as a means of self expression and communication

- Developing aural discrimination and awareness of rhythm and pattern

- Encouraging imaginative and creative play

- Encouraging observation of detail through interaction with an adult.

Physical experiences can be about:

- Giving children opportunity to develop physical confidence and expertise

- Encouraging children to learn about themselves and their perception of themselves

- Being able to judge risk

- Developing manipulative and motor skills, both gross and fine

- Developing balance and co-ordination

- Encouraging knowledge of how bodies work

- Establishing positive attitudes towards an active and healthy way of life

- Becoming aware of parts of one's body and the effects of exercise.

Technological experiences can be about:

- Developing curiosity about objects and materials in the environment

- Responding to needs created through imaginative play

- Organising, re-organising and using the immediate environment

- Encouraging children to be inventive

- Allowing opportunity for understanding, estimating and calculating possibilities.

Scientific experiences can be about:

- Opportunities to explore and observe the properties of living beings and non-living material

- Developing skills of investigation, questioning, experimenting and problem solving

- Recording findings in a way which is relevant to the children's stage of development

- Developing an awareness of scientific language through concrete experiences

- Having opportunities for sensory/tactile awareness

- Appreciating cause and effect relationships and the consequent changes in state.

Mathematical experiences can be about:

- Developing an awareness of mathematical ideas through active involvement with the physical self and the world of shape and space

- Developing mathematical language

- Recognising and encouraging problem solving in different contexts

- Encouraging an awareness of different patterns, making connections and identifying relationships

- Providing opportunity for experiences with numbers including counting, ordering and measuring

- Allowing opportunity for understanding, estimating and calculating probabilities

- Developing an awareness of maths through exploration of everyday materials and equipment.

Linguistic and literacy experiences can be about:

- Developing children's speaking and listening skills

- Exposing children to a range of different styles of language use

- Encouraging high quality dialogue between child/child and adult/child

- Using language in many forms

- Encouraging children to have confidence in themselves as speakers, early writers and readers

- Helping children to realise that books are enjoyable and satisfying

- Nurturing a long lasting interest in books

- Encouraging an awareness that books can be informative and instructional as well as telling stories

- Extending children's ability to listen, speak and write in a meaningful way

- Helping children to understand that reading and writing are part of the communication process

- Developing motivation and interest in reading and writing.

Personal and social experiences can be about:

- Developing an awareness of self and others

- Playing cooperatively with others

- Sharing experiences, ideas and equipment

- Encouraging interaction with other children and adults

- Developing a sense of reliability and responsibility towards equipment, materials and other people

- Developing independence, personal autonomy and making choices and decisions that determine their own learning

- Understanding the passing of time – relating to past, present and future events

- Developing a caring attitude and responsibility for nature and the environment

- Providing the opportunity for challenge, risk and humour.

Cohort progress analysis example

Day Nursery – 0-2 year olds room	**2 March 2017**

Details of areas and/or aspects where there are differences in the progress children are making:

Samuel – Managing feelings and behaviour and speaking

Daisy – Managing feelings and behaviour

Ellie – Managing feelings and behaviour

Ryan – speaking

Jake – all prime areas* (key concern all areas 8-20 mths, age 28 months)

Esme – all prime areas

Details of areas and/or aspects where generally children are making more or less progress:
35.7% of children are making less progress in the aspect managing feelings and behaviour

Conclusions:
Staff to reflect on how managing feelings and behaviour are supported in the room.

Action necessary as a result of the analysis:
Jake – put in place a clear plan of how to support his development in all prime areas and discuss with parents.

Esme – put in place a clear plan of how to support his development in all prime areas and discuss with parents.

Samuel – identify strategies to support language development to limit frustration which is affecting behaviour.

Review of development matters for 8-20 months and 16-26 months for managing feelings and behaviour, consider how this is supported within the room and ensure practitioners are aware of progress children are making and that this is reflected in observations and assessement. Put in place an action plan.

Expected impact of action
Children to make more progress in the aspect managing feelings and behaviour.

Clear progress in the prime areas of learning for Jake and Esme.

Completed by:	**Date:**

Cohort percentage analysis example

Date Percentage of children in different groups achieving above or below their age bracket.					
Area of learning and aspect	**BOYS**	**GIRLS**	**SEN**	**EAL**	**EYPP**
PSED: Making Relationships					
PSED: Self Confidence and Self Awareness					
PSED: Managing Feelings and Behaviour					
CL: Listening and Attention					
CL: Understanding					
CL: Speaking					
PD: Health and Self Care					
PD: Moving and Handling					
L: Reading					
L: Writing					
M: Numbers					
M: Shape, Space and Measure					
UW: People and Communities					
UW: The World					
UW: Technology					
EAD: Exploring Media and Materials					
EAD: Being Imaginative					
EVALUATION:					
KEY AREAS FOR DEVELOPMENT:					

Reflective practice chart

Consider your key children, and where you think the edge of their capabilities might be. Reflect on what they enjoy, their development and the characteristics of effective learning.

Child	Where might the edge of their capabilities be?		How to challenge	

PHOTOCOPIABLE   Quality of teaching, learning and assessment in the EYFS

Impact on learning indicators

It is essential to consider the impact of what you do on children's learning and development. Think about teaching and learning in the book area.

Teaching	Impact on learning
Role models how to handle books carefully and read from left to right and top to bottom.	Children learn how to hold books the correct way up and turn pages independently to follow a story. They gain an understanding of how to treat books with respect.
Models language and introduces new words.	Children's range of vocabulary is extended, reflecting the breadth of their experiences.
Actively listens and responds to children's thoughts.	Develops children's understanding of turn taking, pausing, listening to others, and positively builds and deepens relationships. A genuine response shows them that their opinions, ideas, thoughts and feelings matter.
Asks a high number of closed questions.	Closed questions do not require the child to actively engage in the conversation and they can become disengaged.
Poses open-ended questions and gives time for children to process questions and reply. What if... I wonder... How did... Why did... What happened.	Encourages children to use language. Instead of just answering "yes" or "no". Children need to give fuller responses that draw on a wider range of vocabulary. Time enables children to process questions and put their thoughts into words.
Accurately matches stories to the interests and learning needs of children.	Children are more motivated and eager to join in. As a result, all children make good progress in relation to their starting points.
Varies intonation, pitch, tone, speed and volume to create interest and variety, and to express emotions such as delight, anger, surprise or worry.	Ignites children's interest which supports their listening and attention skills. Provides children with an understanding of emotional language.
Uses repetition and gives children opportunities to listen to the language of the story more than once.	Reinforces key vocabulary and phrases and enables children to consolidate their learning or develop new interests. With each re-telling, children become more confident and fluent in using the language the story contains.
Points to illustrations in the book.	Helps children associate sounds, words and meanings, as well as make connections in the ways different elements in the story relate to each other.
Has a wide range of books, including fact, fiction, rhymes, dual language, sensory books, picture and sound books attractively presented and easily accessible.	Children explore books independently raising their awareness of different scripts and they begin to understand that print carries meaning. Children with EAL feel valued and develop a sense of belonging as their home language is reflected in the environment.
Uses supporting props and visual cues effectively during story times and these are made available for children to access in the environment.	Children demonstrate higher engagement levels and are active participants in their own learning. They develop their imaginative skills as they re-tell stories and create their own narratives in play.

Source: Northamptonshire Early Years.

Lesson observation

Practitioner/Teacher:_____ Observer:_____

Date:_____ Time: _____ Class/Room:_____

ATTITUDE AND APPROACH ■ Positive relationships with children ■ Demonstrates high expectations ■ Models positive attitude and behaviour	
KNOWLEDGE AND UNDERSTANDING ■ Clear understanding and knowledge of the EYFS	
PLANNING AND TEACHING ■ Reflective of interests and learning needs ■ Opportunity to extend learning ■ Responsive to children ■ Builds on previous knowledge ■ Appropriate teaching methods and styles ■ Models and uses language appropriate for the children's stage of development ■ Behaviour management ■ Range of resources and teaching methods ■ Supports self esteem ■ Supports children to reflect	

Points for discussion and reflection

Planning and expectations	
Teaching	
Children's learning	

PHOTOCOPIABLE   Quality of teaching, learning and assessment in the EYFS

References

- *Assessing Quality in Early Childhood Education and Care: Sustained Shared Thinking and Emotional Well Being (SSTEW) Scale for 2-5 year olds provision.* Siraj, I et al (2015) IOE Press

- *Development Matters* (DfE 2012)

- *Early Years Inspection Handbook* (Ofsted September 2015)

- *First Steps Outdoors: Making the most of your Outdoor Space* (Young Wales)

- *How Children Learn: The Characteristics of Effective Learning.* Stewart, N (2011) BAECE

- *Learning, Playing and Interacting* (DCSF 2009)

- Northamptonshire Early Years: www.northamptonshire.gov.uk/eyfs

- Resources to Support Outdoor Learning Experiences: https://www.herefordshire.gov.uk/media/7674712/outdoorprovisionaudit3.pdf

- *Teaching and Play in the Early Years: A Balancing Act* (Ofsted June 2015)

- *Time to Play in Early Childhood Education.* Bruce, T (1991) Hodder and Stoughton

Acknowledgements

This book would not have been possible, were it not for all the wonderful and interesting practitioners I meet through my training and consultancy work. You all enable me to reflect, consider and think about best practice in early years and how to share those thoughts with you.

Special thanks are due to:

Zoe Wright, Operations Director, Magic Nurseries;

Tracey Heayns and her team at Busy Bees Montessori Nursery, Rushden, Northamptonshire;

Debbie Styles and her team at Lord William's School Day Nursery, Thame, Oxfordshire;

Louise Brooks, Amanda Chenery and their team at The Nursery, Oxford;

Fran Mullan and her team at The Secret Garden Pre School, Princes Risborough, Buckinghamshire.

These settings all welcomed me to come and observe freely their excellent provision, which then informed many of the good practice examples in this book.